Booming from the Mists of Nowhere

A BUR OAK BOOK

Holly Carver, series editor

Booming from the Mists of Nowhere

The Story of the Greater Prairie-Chicken

BY GREG HOCH

University of Iowa Press, Iowa City

University of Iowa Press, Iowa City 52242
Copyright © 2015 by the University of Iowa Press
www.uiowapress.org
Printed in the United States of America

Design by Kristina Kachele Design, llc

The University of Iowa Press is a member of Green Press Initiative
and is committed to preserving natural resources.

Printed on acid-free paper

Library of Congress Cataloging-in-Publication Data
Hoch, Greg, 1971–
Booming from the mists of nowhere : the story of the greater prairie-chicken / by Greg Hoch.
pages   cm. — (A bur oak book)
Includes bibliographical references and index.
ISBN 978-1-60938-387-9 (pbk), ISBN 978-1-60938-388-6 (ebk)
1. Greater prairie chicken.   I. Title.
QL696.G27H62   2015

598.6—dc23   2015008711

To Dave

and

to Jean and Mary

There is a peculiar virtue in the music of elusive birds. Songsters that sing from top-most boughs are easily seen and as easily forgotten; they have the mediocrity of the obvious. What one remembers is the invisible hermit thrush pouring silver chords from impenetrable shadows; the soaring crane trumpeting from behind a cloud; the prairie chicken booming from the mists of nowhere; the quail's Ave Maria in the hush of dawn.
—Aldo Leopold, *A Sand County Almanac*

Contents

Acknowledgments

Carmelita, Mike, Bob, Bill, and Paul, thanks for all your help and support at my job. Commissioner Landwehr, thanks for being such a tireless advocate for grass. I also want to thank everyone at the Detroit Lakes Wetland Management District office, especially the gang out in the firehouse. I appreciate you letting me drag a drip torch along with you guys. Becky, thanks for putting up with my daily crazy ideas. Scott, Cathy, and Ryan have all taught me a lot. Jim, thanks for all you've done for Minnesota's prairies.

I would also like to thank the rest of my friends and colleagues in the Minnesota Department of Natural Resources, US Fish and Wildlife Service, The Nature Conservancy, Pheasants Forever, and all the other conservation organizations out there who work daily to preserve, protect, and manage prairies. Without their tireless work, there would be a lot less prairie. I especially want to thank those members of the Minnesota Prairie Chicken Society and the Wildlife Society. No story about the prairie-chicken could be complete without a tip of the hat to John Toepfer.

I also need to thank the group at Konza Prairie, especially John, who introduced me to the intricacies of the prairie at every level, from atoms to organisms to ecosystems.

I would also like to thank all the editorial staff at the University of Iowa Press who helped shepherd this project from conception to completion.

Thanks to Deanna, Mom, and Dad for putting up with me. Last, thanks to Boomer, who reminds me daily to put down the pen, turn off the computer, and go walk in the prairie.

Preface

This book has three goals. The first is to introduce readers to a somewhat neglected member of a somewhat neglected ecosystem, the greater prairie-chicken and the tallgrass prairie. The prairie-chicken played a key role in the settlement of the Midwest. This book will place this species into a historical context. Some have argued that the prairie-chicken, perhaps along with deer, was a key species in the diet and economic life of many settlers. Many pioneer families might have starved during the winter without prairie-chicken dinners. Sending prairie-chickens to eastern markets probably kept a few farms and farmers solvent during hard times. Prairie-chicken hunting drew many eastern hunters to the Midwest.

The second goal is to introduce some of the basic concepts of population, community, and landscape ecology, as well as conservation biology and wildlife management, using prairie-chickens and tallgrass prairie as examples. Wildlife and habitat management is complex, as are processes such as evolution and ecology. Because this book is meant for a general audience, I tried to simplify these complexities and avoid scientific jargon. I hope the science is still evident.

Third, and more than anything, this book is my way of catching up. One of the most intimidating places for me is a board meeting of the Minnesota Prairie Chicken Society. Many of the people sitting around the table have been managing prairie habitat and prairie wildlife since I was rather young. Researching this bird, its history, and its management is my way of trying to keep up with them and contribute something to the conversation.

This book is not intended to be a technical treatment or a scientific review of the latest research in tallgrass prairie or prairie-chicken ecology, conservation, or management. There are a number of both types of books already written. More technical or more detailed information about prairie-chickens can be found in *The Grouse of the World* and *Grassland Grouse and Their Conservation*, both by Paul Johnsgard; *Adaptive Strategies and Population Ecology of Northern Grouse*, volumes 1 and 2, edited by Arthur Bergerud and Michael Gratson; *Ecology, Conservation, and Management of Grouse*, edited by Brett Sandercock, Kathy Martin, and Gernot Segelbacher; and *The Greater Prairie Chicken: A National Look*, edited by Dan Svedarsky, Ross Hier, and Nova Silvy.

There are numerous quotations throughout this book. Some are from the recent scientific literature. However, the majority come from pioneer and early settler accounts of the tallgrass prairie region and from some of the early hunters who harvested astounding numbers of these birds. I also relied heavily on some of the earlier research about wildlife from the first half of the twentieth century. All too often it is easy to overlook this older literature in favor of what was published most recently. Many of these early writings have a poetry to them that is sadly lacking in much of today's literature. Instead of trying to summarize or paraphrase, I used their direct quotes in the hope of letting their stories come through and giving them a voice in this book.

I also hope that this book inspires people to become more involved in the prairie. Take a family vacation to chicken country and spend an April morning in a blind watching the males' courtship dance. Become active in a local conservation group. Search for and hand-pick prairie seeds in ditches, old cemeteries, or wherever else you can find them and help restore some prairie near you. If you are interested in helping prairie-chickens and other prairie wildlife, please consider joining the North American Grouse Partnership, the Minnesota Prairie Chicken Society, the Society of Tympanuchus Cupido Pinnatus in Wisconsin, and state or national groups concerned with prairie conservation in general.

A book of this type will never be complete. There's always one more forgotten historical article to read, one more person to talk to and story to hear, one more data sheet at the bottom of a file cabinet somewhere. This book is just a start at someday telling the full story of the prairie and prairie-chicken. I apologize to all the writers and researchers who were not cited in this book. It seems like I left out one or two papers for every citation included.

Booming from the Mists of Nowhere

CHAPTER 1

The Greater Prairie-Chicken

The pinnated grouse, commonly known as the prairie chicken,
is the most conspicuous member of the grouse family, and
has been more intimately associated with the development
of our country than any other game bird. —*Bruette 1916*

They were the most beautiful poultry imaginable. When we awoke
in the morning to the sweet music of their mating calls, we knew it
was time to clean the wheat for the spring sowing. —*Quick 1925*

The history of the prairie chicken has no equal in the whole
American outdoor picture. It is the story of America's finest
native grouse, its finest native game bird—perhaps the out-
standing subject in all American wildlife. —*Dalrymple 1950*

In those days, during the winter, the grouse would enter the
farmyards and feed with the poultry, alight on the houses
or walk the very streets of the villages. —*Audubon 1831*

On a map of the United States, the land of the tallgrass prairie lies at
the country's center. It is the heart of the nation. "The prairie, in all
its expressions, is a massive subtle place, with a long history of con-
tradictions and misunderstanding. But it is worth the effort at com-
prehension. It is, after all, the center of our national identity" (Fields
1888, quoted in Least Heat-Moon 1991).

If the prairie is at the center of our national identity, the
prairie-chicken is at the center of the prairie. The bison, or buffalo, is

the characteristic species of the presettlement prairies. However, by the time most settlers arrived on the prairie, the bison were a memory. The prairie-chicken is the iconic species of the settlement period.

The prairie-chicken has been described as a rather drab, predominantly brown bird, and it *is* a rather drab bird that is almost doomed by its common name. Its proper name is the pinnated grouse. While "grouse" brings to mind images of noble birds inhabiting beautiful landscapes, "chicken" makes a person think of Grandma's casserole. It's also hard to generate conservation interest in a drab brown chicken.

For ten months of the year, the prairie-chickens' cryptic colors allow them to disappear into the landscape.

> The prairie chicken is a child of the sullen winter grasses, dappled brown like a winter prairie field, so that when this wild thing lies close along the grass, an expert eye might forgive itself for not beholding it. (Quayle 1905)

> It is a bird the color of autumn grasses, its feathers disruptively patterned in vertical stripes of switchgrass buff and Indiangrass brown, so that a motionless prairie-chicken simply fades into the background. (Johnsgard 2014)

However, during the other two months, April and May, it is one of the most outrageously flamboyant birds in North America.

> The male is at this season attired in his full dress, and enacts his part in a manner not surpassed in pomposity by any other bird. (Audubon 1831)

This leaves us with a bird that is pompously drab or drably pompous.

The greater prairie-chicken belongs to the order of birds called the Galliformes and to the family Phasianidae. Gallinaceous birds include grouse, ptarmigan, pheasant, quail, and turkey.

The greater prairie-chicken goes by several names. Its proper name, pinnated grouse, comes from the pinnae, tall feathers the male erects on his neck when displaying for females. The scientific name is *Tympanuchus cupido pinnatus*. *Tympanuchus* is a reference to the deep, booming sound the males make on their leks, or booming grounds, in the spring. Think timpani drums. *Cupido* is a reference to the pinnae on the neck. These feathers reminded early taxonomists of the wings of Cupid. *Pinnatus* is of course a reference to the pinnae.

Prairie chickens were commonly noted by the earliest of European explorers. Father Marquette has the distinction of being the first European to encounter the prairie chicken in the region [Chicago] and perhaps the first anywhere to describe it. The priest records in his entry of December 12, 1674, that "Jacques brought a partridge which he had killed, quite similar to that of France, except that it had, as it were, two little wings of three or four feathers a finger long near the head which cover the neck where there are no feathers." It is, in fact, these little appendages of feathers, thought by Linnaeus to resemble the wings of a Roman god, that give the bird its Latin name of *cupido*. (Greenberg 2002)

Other names include prairie hen and Ol' Muldoon, an onomatopoetic interpretation of the males' spring call. Some call it kettledrummer for the deep sound of its booming. Young-of-the-year were called yellowlegs because their legs were not yet feathered. Hunters often referred to them as squaretails, to differentiate them from the similar sharp-tailed grouse.

The greater prairie-chicken has several very close relatives. The heath hen (*Tympanuchus cupido cupido*) of the East Coast and the Attwater's prairie-chicken (*Tympanuchus cupido attwateri*) of the coastal prairies of Louisiana and eastern Texas are also considered subspecies. Some suspect that it was heath hen served at the first Thanksgiving, instead of or in addition to the traditional turkey. Heath hen was considered a delicacy.

It is somewhat extraordinary that European naturalists, in their various accounts of our different species of Grouse, should have said little or nothing of the one now before us [heath hen], which, in its voice, manners, and peculiarity of plumage, is the most singular, and, in its flesh, the most excellent of all those of its tribe that inhabit the territory of the United States. (Wilson 1839)

This bird occurred in vast flocks on the Eastern Seaboard, and eventually the early settlers had too much of a good thing. As they moved across the Appalachian Mountains, they brought this bias with them:

When I first moved to Kentucky, the Pinnated Grouse were so abundant, that they were held in no higher estimation as food than the most common flesh, and no "hunter of Kentucky" deigned to shoot them. My own servants preferred the fattest flitch of bacon to their flesh, and not unfrequently laid them aside as unfit for cooking. (Audubon 1831)

As immigrants settled the Midwest over the next century, prairie-chickens continued to play an important role in their diet. The prairie-chicken may have done more than any other species to feed people, and in some cases keep them alive, through the winter.

Prairie chickens probably contributed more to homesteaders than the buffalo ever did. (Horak 1985)

At 10–12 years old, I was enthralled by Grandpa O. Helmer Johnson's talk about his "helping" move his uncle from Fertile [Minnesota] to Hillsboro, ND. It was about 1910 and he was 10–11 years old. They were travelling in horse drawn wagons and when meal time came he and the other kids would go out in front of the horses with a stick and knock down enough "chickens" to cook up for that meal. I'm quite sure this was in July or Aug, and the Chickens were fledglings, perhaps 3/4 grown and "fryin size". Hard to imagine how abundant they must have been. (Earl Johnson, pers. comm. 2011)

By 1929 there was only a single male heath hen left on Martha's Vineyard. In 1932 he disappeared. The heath hen, along with the passenger pigeon, is one of the few avian species humanity has actually watched as it became extinct.

The Attwater's prairie-chicken is named after an English naturalist who specialized in the birds of southern Texas. In 1998, only 56 birds existed in the wild (Silvy, Peterson, and Lopez 2004). According to the title of a 2002 story about these birds in *National Geographic* magazine, the species was "down to a handful." By March 2009, fewer than 100 birds were known to be living in the wild. Another 135 lived in multiple captive-breeding facilities and research centers. The wild birds were located at the Attwater Prairie Chicken National Wildlife Refuge, the Texas City Prairie Preserve, and several private ranches in Goliad County, Texas (Morrow et al. 2010).

The lesser prairie-chicken (*Tympanuchus pallidicinctus*), a distinct species, is found on the southwestern edge of the greater prairie-chicken's modern range, in the general area where Oklahoma, Texas, Kansas, New Mexico, and Colorado meet. At the beginning of the twenty-first century, some conservationists are lobbying for the species to be listed as threatened or endangered under the Endangered Species Act. The two other grassland grouse, more distantly related, are the sharp-tailed grouse (*Tympanuchus phasianellus*) and the sage-grouse. The sage-grouse was recently divided into two species, the greater sage-grouse (*Centrocercus urophasianus*) and the Gunnison sage-grouse (*Centrocercus minimus*).

While the sage-grouse is a very distinct-looking bird living well west of the prairie-chicken's range, there is often confusion between the prairie-chicken and sharp-tailed grouse. When reading old hunting accounts, one needs to be careful in determining what species of prairie grouse was being hunted. Often the birds were simply lumped together.

The term "prairie chicken" is here used in the same sense as it is used by most sportsmen, namely, as inclusive of both pinnated and sharp-tailed grouse. (Leopold 1931)

> At the present time there is no attempt to separate sharp-tailed
> grouse from greater pinnated grouse harvested in South Dakota or
> Nebraska. (M. Johnson and Knue 1989)

At the northern extent of the range, "prairie-chicken" historically referred to the sharp-tailed grouse, while "prairie hen" referred to the pinnated grouse (Houston 2002).

Issues like these require us to be detectives when reading the historical literature. In his tour of the Minnesota River Valley in 1835, George Featherstonhaugh (1847) records several observations. Just downriver of Mankato, Minnesota, in the south-central part of the state, he describes a "large brood of heavy grouse (*Tetrao cupido*)." *Tetrao* was the original name of the *Tympanuchus* genus. The *cupido* species name clearly indicates that this was a record of prairie-chickens, not sharp-tails. Mankato would have been slightly outside the range of this species at the time (see chapter 5). As Featherstonhaugh continues north and west up the river into west-central Minnesota, he records "*Tetrao* . . . heavy birds weighing about 2 lb. each" and "*Tetrao* . . . so large and fat, that they looked like barn-door fowl." These records would have been well outside the assumed range of prairie-chickens.

Earlier in his travels, Featherstonhaugh described *Tetrao cupido*, prairie-chickens, as "heavy grouse." In west-central Minnesota, he described only *Tetrao*, which could be either prairie-chickens or sharp-tails. The fact that he called them "heavy" implies that he was talking about prairie-chickens, but we cannot be sure. If these were chickens, it would expand the presettlement range of this species to the northwest significantly.

> The sharp-tail is a habitat generalist; it is not nearly as particular
> about specific habitat types. Sharp-tails do well in grassland, shru-
> bland, and forest clearings. Today the sharp-tail ranges from northern
> Wisconsin almost to the West Coast and northward to central Alaska.
> However, during settlement the sharp-tail was not nearly as tolerant
> of American agriculture. While the prairie-chicken expanded north
> and west with the plow, the sharp-tail contracted in front of the plow.

It [sharp-tail] is however, essentially a bird of the wilds, and it is a curious fact that it seems to retreat before civilization, continually moving west as the wheat fields advance, while its place is taken by the common form [prairie chicken], which seems to keep pace with settlement. (Roosevelt 1899)

The pinnated grouse, or true prairie chicken, is very fond of cultivated fields, of wheat, kaffir, and corn, but the sharptail clings to his native hills, living today as he did when he and the buffalo had a common range in the Northwest. (Askins 1931)

In contrast to sharp-tailed grouse, which are largely dependent on wild land, the bulk of Michigan's prairie chicken population today is associated with privately-owned agricultural lands. (Ammann 1957)

Sharp-tailed grouse and prairie-chickens are so closely related that there are reports of hybrids in the scientific literature. Johnsgard and Wood (1968) reported hybrids from seven states and four provinces. They estimated that between 0.3 and 1.2 percent of the population were hybrids of the two species.

The three other grouse-like birds that now inhabit parts of the midwestern grasslands are the ring-necked pheasant (*Phasianus colchinus*), Hungarian or gray partridge (*Perdix perdix*), and chukar (*Alectoris chukar*). All three of these birds were introduced from Europe or Asia, and today they are probably more popular among hunters than the native birds.

The prairie-chicken is often overlooked. One report from Indiana in the 1950s stated that

there was no public interest to save the chicken, and reflecting back on the extinction of the chicken one is filled with regret, as part of our heritage is gone. They could have been saved, but there was neither the demand or outcry to save them. In 1958 one high state official—I won't tell you his name—told me "Madden, shoot a cock and a hen, mount them, put them in the State Museum, if people want to see a prairie chicken." (quoted in S. Jones 1992)

A second report, from the *Sleepy Eye Herald Dispatch* in Minnesota in April 1973, stated that

the status and future of Minnesota's prairie chicken will be the subject of a conference in Crookston. Jim Putnam, editor of the *Granite Falls Tribune*, thinks it's pure folly to call such a meeting. He says there has been no open season on prairie chickens since 1942. The population began to decline sharply as the acreage of cultivated land increased, grasslands disappeared and land owners converted their wheat fields to corn and soybean. Putnam says he grew up with a .410 shotgun and has never killed or even seen a prairie chicken. Said he: "We haven't seen any zebras running around the acres either. The chickens have flown the coop and the meeting at Crookston is just another reason why Minnesota taxes are among the highest in the world." (quoted in Svedarsky, Wolfe, and Toepfer 1999)

The prairie-chicken is not a wilderness bird. It can do quite well around people, their farms, and even small towns and cities.

Prairie chickens are very plenty in the city now. Every morning hundreds of them are flying about, skimming along over barns, darting past the house doors and alighting on garden fences. (quoted in Schorger 1944)

On 27 October 1879, six migrating prairie chickens perched on the rooftop of the German Methodist Church in Madison, and took a look at the growing city. (Leopold 1949)

Often, they came even closer, right into the yard.

They do not retire as the country becomes settled, but continue to lurk in the tall grass around the newly made farms; and I have sometimes seen them mingled with the domestic fowls, a short distance from the farmer's door. (Van Tramp 1868)

They came in from the prairie to feed with the tame hens, alighted on the roofs of the shack before daylight, followed the plow and dusted in the furrows, watered at the horse-troughs, and scratched in the gardens like veritable brown leghorns. (Askins 1931)

Some hunters even preferred these more domesticated birds.

Its flavor is much affected by what it feeds on, and in this part of the country where its principal food is rosebuds, is not nearly so good as in civilized districts, where it eats Indian corn by wholesale. (Palliser 1853)

However, with changing land-use practices, including the conversion of diverse prairie to monoculture corn, their populations plummeted. At one point, some of the leading wildlife experts in the nation were ready to give up on the prairie-chicken.

To-day the Prairie-Chicken is to be numbered with the buffalo and the passenger pigeon. It is useless to describe this bird. The chances are that no reader of this book will ever see one outside of a museum. (Hornaday 1904)

Is the prairie chicken hopeless? (Leopold 1931)

Another reason the prairie-chicken disappeared, or was allowed to disappear, was a newcomer that stole the hearts of America's hunters. That newcomer was the ring-necked pheasant. It liked the new rural landscape and could be easily mass-produced.

The prairie chicken is difficult to artificially propagate on game farms. Our thinking on these questions has been muddled by the automatic assumption that to produce game we must buy stock and confine it in chicken-wire slums for breeding and subsequent release. Pheasants tolerate slums, but quail barely, and the lordly chicken not at all. (Leopold 1999)

However, not everyone saw the trade-off between the prairie-chicken and the pheasant as positive.

There are good grounds for questioning the wisdom of spending thousands of dollars in an effort to introduce foreign game birds, which, at most, are but game chickens, when we have a noble game bird, native to our soil that simply asks for a living chance to repopulate our prairies, marshes, and cornfields. (Bruette 1916)

Prairie-chickens are, admittedly, not the easiest species to manage for. Few people would want to exclude pheasants from the prairie-chicken's range. With enough grass and proper habitat management, however, there is room on the prairie landscape for many species of grassland birds.

CHAPTER 2

The Prairie

Loneliness, thy other name, thy one true
synonym, is prairie. —*Quayle 1905*

Between that earth and that sky I felt erased, blotted out. I did not say
my prayers that night: here, I felt, what would be would be. —*Cather 1918*

Every American has the right as part of his cultural heritage to stand in
grass as high as his head in order to feel some small measure of history
coursing through his veins. —*Elder 1961, quoted in Least Heat-Moon 1991*

I have seen the golden plover, or prairie pigeon, running over
the new-burned prairie in such numbers that the earth seemed
to be moving, as with their black bellies and beautiful gold
and silver spangles they sought their food. —*Quick 1925*

Any discussion of the prairie-chicken must begin, as the bird's name
begins, with the prairie. The prairie is a land of sky and grass, meeting
at an infinite horizon. The horizon is the most visually simple landscape you can find outside of the ocean. Looking down at your feet,
at the dozens of grasses and wildflowers and hundreds of insects, you
will find one of the most complex tapestries imaginable.

Prairie is a uniquely North American ecosystem. South America has
its pampas, Asia its steppes, Africa its veldt. But the prairies belong
to North America. The word "prairie" came through French from the
Latin *pratum*, meaning "meadow." A meadow is generally thought of
as a small opening in a forest, but this was an opening in the eastern
forest that stretched past the infinite horizon.

The tallgrass prairie formed a rough triangle in the center of the country. When discussing the prairie, most people turn to Edgar Transeau's 1935 map of the prairie peninsula. On this map the prairie-forest border starts around the Michigan-Indiana border and stretches in a ragged line to southeastern Kansas. To the northwest the prairie-forest edge runs through the middle of Wisconsin and continues to the junction of Minnesota, North Dakota, and Manitoba.

The prairie is defined and maintained by three factors: grazing, fire, and climate. The prairie is a diverse ecosystem, but it is structurally simple. In the forest, plants can grow in the herbaceous, sapling, and canopy layers, stretching up from the ground sometimes hundreds of feet. Other plants, known as epiphytes, can grow on the branches of the taller trees, most famously in the rain forests. Animals, notably insects and birds, specialize in living in each of these layers.

In the prairie, most plants can grow to only a few feet above the ground. Almost every species has to pack into that small space, making the prairie a very competitive environment. It's even more competitive belowground: 90 percent of the living material, or biomass, in the prairie—plant, animal, fungal, bacterial—lives below the soil surface.

By some theories, all else being equal, there should be one species that can outcompete and eliminate all the others over time. In the prairie, big bluestem (*Andropogon gerardii*) would be a good candidate for this supercompetitor. Big bluestem grows by tillering under the soil and sending up new shoots from rhizomes. One clump of bluestem with many stems may be connected underground by one root system and is in fact a single organism. As those tillers move outward, they can use the energy and resources from the center of the plant. This gives them a strong competitive advantage and should allow them to crowd out neighboring plants of other species.

The reason this doesn't happen is that disturbances knock back the most dominant or competitive species or individuals. Some species do well during a cool, wet summer versus a hot, dry summer. Some species do well immediately after a fire, while others do best several years after the last fire. Species respond both positively and negatively to grazing. With all these different disturbances interacting on the landscape across space and time, and different species reacting differently to those disturbances, no one species is able to crowd out all others, and diversity is maintained.

When we think of grazers, we picture large, brown, furry animals. However, in terms of overall biomass and amount of plant material eaten, we may want to picture small, green, chitinous creatures, such as grasshoppers, leafhoppers, and hundreds of other insect species. Or we may want to think of nematodes and other microscopic organisms both above and below the soil surface.

Most grazers target a specific group of plants in their diet. Bison and cattle both strongly prefer grasses over wildflowers, or forbs, as they are more appropriately known (Plumb and Dodd 1993). Their grazing removes the dominant plants—grasses—and makes room for the forbs. Well-managed grazing increases plant diversity, sometimes almost doubling it (Vinton et al. 1993; Hickman et al. 2004; Towne, Hartnett, and Cochran 2005).

Grazers also alter the structure of the vegetation. An ungrazed prairie appears homogeneous, a continuous canopy of evenly spaced bluestem seedheads waving in the wind. In a grazed prairie, some areas will be heavily grazed and some lightly grazed, while other areas will show little sign of grazing. This creates a heterogeneous landscape. In these areas, there is habitat for grassland birds and other wildlife that prefer all types of nesting cover and foraging habitat.

Grazers have other effects on the prairie. And here we should expand "grazing" to include animal disturbances more generally. Bison wallow, creating small wetlands after rainstorms. Hoof action crushes some plants. Urination and defecation change the fertility of the soil at small scales, making the prairie even more heterogeneous. Burrowing animals create holes and mounds of bare dirt, providing loose fertile soil, ideal for seed germination. Soil invertebrates aerate the soil with their tunnels.

Fire, another disturbance in the tallgrass prairie, has several effects on the plants and animals. First, it removes the insulating detritus, or buildup, of previous years' dead stems. This, in addition to the black ash left behind, warms the soil in the spring. Unburned prairie can stay quite cold, even frozen, well into the spring. Second, fire volatilizes nitrogen. While some nutrients, such as phosphorus, return to the soil in the ash, nitrogen literally goes up in smoke.

Because of the soil warming and direct sunlight on the soil surface, fires generally stimulate both plant growth and flowering. Productivity, the amount of plant material or biomass produced, will almost always be higher in burned prairies compared to unburned (Briggs and Knapp 1995). Anyone who has spent any time in the prairie knows how well most plants flower in the summer following a fire. If fires occur too late in the spring, early-emerging species such as pasqueflower can be affected that year. Periodic fires, even late in the spring, probably do minimal damage to these species. Overall, almost all prairie plant species will respond positively to fire.

Many animals also respond positively to fire. Grazers will almost always prefer to graze on burned prairie compared to unburned prairie (Fuhlendorf and Engle 2004). Early spring fires can remove nesting cover for birds, while late spring fires can destroy nests. However, grassland birds are good renesters. Fires will also remove cover for small mammals such as mice and voles. It's not unusual during fires to see dozens of hawks, especially Swainson's hawks, circling overhead, looking for a freshly exposed meal.

There are three key questions to ask concerning grassland fire: Were the fires natural, started by lightning, or started by humans? How often did they occur? And in what season did most fires occur historically?

In the western Rockies, lightning storms, despite what Smokey the Bear says, start most fires. But in the more humid eastern tallgrass prairie region, torrential rains usually accompany lightning storms. While lightning fires do occur in the tallgrass region, they are relatively rare. As far as fire frequency, there are scores of references in the historical literature to annual or very frequent fires (Pyne 1982; Stewart 2002; Courtwright 2011).

We can learn several things from these historical accounts. First, prairie fires were probably more common than prescribed fires are today. Second, because lightning fires are rare, we must conclude that humans started the vast majority of these fires: "The Indians within the entire circuit of their possessions set fire to the dry grass of the prairie, and the flame with incredible rapidity spreads over the country" (Ernst 1903). Finally, we can conclude that early explorers probably exaggerated somewhat, or at least extrapolated local observations to regional patterns. While fire was common, not every acre could have burned every year. This was the time when flights of ducks darkened the sky. If all the nesting cover was removed every year, where were all those nests?

Today, the majority of prescribed fires in the tallgrass region are conducted in April and May. McClain and Elzinga (1994) reviewed the historical literature from the tallgrass prairie region and found that the majority of fires before Euro-American settlement were in the fall. "After the prairies are burnt off, an event which usually happened sometime in October, golden plovers would visit them in vast numbers" (Wall 1894). The reason Native Americans burned in the fall was to herd animals during hunts (Bakeless 1950).

The fact that these fires were in the fall gives more credence to the human versus lightning origins of fire. In the Midwest, most thunderstorms are in the spring and summer. If lightning were the primary ignition source, those historic fires would not have been in the fall. From the historical literature, we can conclude that prairie fires were set by humans, in the fall, at fairly high frequencies.

Climate, climate variability, and periodic drought constitute the third major disturbance in tallgrass prairie. The world's largest grasslands are always in the center of continents and often in the rain shadow of a mountain range. America's grasslands meet both of these requirements. As warm, moist air moves eastward off the Pacific, it hits several mountain ranges, most notably the Rockies. This warm, moist air is forced upward over the mountains. As the air rises, it cools. Cold air holds less water than warm air. The moisture falls as rain on the windward side of the mountains and the cold, dry air falls down the leeward side of the mountains. As the air moves eastward, it picks up some moisture along the way. This phenomenon explains large-scale grassland patterns in the United States: shortgrass in eastern Colorado, mixed-grass in central Kansas, and tallgrass in Iowa and eastward.

Climate is also highly variable in grasslands because of their location in the center of continents. These areas have no oceans to buffer temperature changes. Seattle, Washington, is roughly the same distance from the equator as Fargo, North Dakota. But Fargo has no large body of water to moderate its climate. Prairie summers can easily reach over one hundred degrees. Prairie winters, especially in the northern plains, frequently drop to thirty or forty below. In Seattle, because of the ocean's moderating effect, there is less daily, seasonal, and annual variability in the climate.

This highly variable climate may partly explain the eastern edge of this ecosystem. Tallgrass prairie has enough precipitation to support trees. However, the area is also subject to periodic severe droughts, like the Dust Bowl of the 1930s (Kunkel et al. 2003). These droughts may knock trees back frequently enough that they are never able to become established enough to form a forest. There were once trees along streams and rivers, and there were oak savannas, especially along the prairie-forest border, but there would have been very few trees in upland prairie.

Scientists debate whether the most significant factor for excluding trees from the prairie was fire or climate, especially periodic droughts. Changnon, Kunkel, and Winstanley (2003) found that the tallgrass prairie region experienced droughts that were 50 to 200 percent more severe than they were in neighboring forested areas. While the trees may invade the prairie during the wet cycles, these periodic droughts would knock them back. Likely, both fire and climate working together kept trees from the prairie.

One problem with tallgrass prairie is that it has no definable boundaries. There are dozens of maps of the tallgrass prairie, and while all generally cover the same area, the edges on almost all of them are different. Grass interdigitated with trees in the east, while tall grasses faded into short grasses to the west. Groves of trees grew in the prairie. Clearings of prairie grew in the forest. During droughts and their accompanying fires, the prairie pushed eastward. During wet periods when rainfall was sufficient to support trees, the forest pushed westward.

Is the tallgrass prairie defined by grass of a certain height? Or is it defined by a certain species or group of species? The iconic species of the ecosystem is big bluestem, but there are also dozens of other grasses and hundreds of wildflowers.

The tallgrass prairie has a north-south temperature or energy gradient. In the north, the growing season is very short and the temperatures are cool. In the south, the climate is hot and dry and the plants are water and heat stressed. In both of these areas the grasses will be waist to chest high, but for opposite reasons. The prairie also has an east-west rainfall or moisture gradient. Kansas receives less rain than Illinois. On the western edge of the prairie, the grasses are water limited. Big bluestem in Kansas and Nebraska will be waist high. In Indiana, Iowa, and Illinois, in a wet year, big bluestem, Indian grass, and cordgrass can reach well over a person's head. "But where the land is moist, it [grass] grows more luxuriantly, and is said to become tall enough to hide from view horse and rider" (Van Tramp 1868).

As the pioneers emerged from the eastern forests in the early 1800s into this strange land, they stopped dead in their tracks at the edge of the prairie. "The children of the American Revolution hesitated forty years at the western edge of the forest because they did not trust the grasslands" (Archer and Bunch 1953). In the forest, the branches overhead protect a person from the sun and driving rain. There is no place to hide on the prairie. All that sky and horizon and emptiness terrified those first settlers. "Between that earth and that sky I felt erased, blotted out. I did not say my prayers that night: here, I felt, what would be would be" (Cather 1918).

The mind-set brought over from Europe was that only soils that could grow trees were fertile and moist enough to grow crops. The first pioneers to reach the area needed what only the forests could provide: lumber for building houses and firewood for cooking and heating. The trees also provided shelter from the weather. Thus, the first settlers were restricted to the forests or forest-prairie border for decades. "For a long time, home base remained in the timber, and familiar forests were laboriously cleared in preference to breaking virgin prairie sod. In Marshall County, Iowa, as late as 1867, prairie was selling for $3 to $10 per acre while timbered lands sold for $30 to $50" (Madson 1982). Imagine the surprise of those first farmers when they saw how well their crops grew in that deep, black prairie loam.

The forest-prairie border provided another benefit: an abundance of wildlife. The place where two ecosystems meet is called an ecotone. These areas usually have a high abundance and diversity of plants and animals. The forest-prairie ecotone has forest species as well as grassland species. Add to those some species that specialize on that edge habitat, and all those species together can have a greater abundance and diversity than would be found in the middle of a large forest or the center of a vast grassland.

The tallgrass prairie is the only ecosystem in North America to be functionally driven to extinction. Over its former range, 99.6 percent of the tallgrass prairie is gone. Prairie once covered 971,000 acres in Wisconsin; today only 4,000 acres remain. Illinois, the "Prairie State," had 8.9 million acres and now has 930 acres; Iowa had 12.5 million acres and now has 12,140; and Minnesota had 7.3 million and now has 30,350. Overall, the loss of tallgrass prairie ranges from 82.6 and 85 percent in Kansas and South Dakota, respectively, to 98 percent in Nebraska and more than 99.5 percent in Illinois, Indiana, Iowa, Minnesota, Missouri, North Dakota, and Wisconsin (Samson and Knopf 1994). The prairie that does remain is on the western, or drier, edge of the tallgrass prairie ecosystem. Much of the true tallgrass prairie of Indiana, Illinois, and eastern Iowa is found in tiny fragments, often in small pioneer cemeteries.

The modern history of the prairie may start, sadly, in 1837. That is the year a thirty-three-year-old Illinois man named John Deere invented the moldboard plow. This contraption was unique in that it scoured the new stainless steel moldboard automatically. Previously, as farmers tried to break the prairie, the soil aggregates and those Gordian knots of prairie roots required the farmer to stop every few feet and manually scrape the soil off the plow face.

Ninety percent of the biomass in the prairie is belowground, in the roots. For every pound of grass the horses and oxen walked through, the plow they pulled behind them had to cut through nine pounds of roots. With the self-scouring moldboard, farmers and their teams could move unfettered through the prairie loam. "As the furrow was cut, there was a constant popping sound, like a volley of tiny pistol shots, caused by the breaking of the tough roots and spurs. This incessant cracking and popping had a slight ring to it, amplified by the tempered steel of the moldboard plow" (Madson 1979).

While the history of the tallgrass prairie is one of destruction, the future may be about creation and restoration. People are beginning to see the value of prairies and their component species. A few large, regional areas of prairie remain, notably the Flint Hills of Kansas and the Loess Hills of Iowa, both on the western edge of the tallgrass region. There are other large tracts of land that can be managed as landscapes. These include Bluestem Prairie in Minnesota and Broken Kettle Grasslands in Iowa, both owned by the Nature Conservancy.

Thousands of people across the Midwest are restoring prairies, from backyard gardens to hundred-acre public wildlife areas. In the past couple of decades, restoration has moved beyond this scale to try to restore functioning landscapes on the scale of thousands of contiguous acres of prairie plants. These larger projects include Neal Smith National Wildlife Refuge in Iowa, Glacial Ridge National Wildlife Refuge in Minnesota, Kankakee in Indiana, and Midewin in Illinois. Note that at these sites we are restoring prairie plants.

What took nature thousands of years to build cannot be re-created by humankind in a few years, a decade, or even a lifetime. Restored prairies usually have only a small fraction of the total number of plants seen in native prairie. We lack the knowledge to restore all the soil invertebrates, bacteria, and fungi, as well as the complex relationships between all these organisms. At the other end of the size spectrum, we lack the political will to restore large migratory herds of bison and elk and the grizzly bears and packs of wolves that fed on them.

That's not to say we aren't trying. Numerous plant and soil ecologists, wildlife managers, biologists, and conservationists are researching ways to increase diversity, studying the interactions of insect and plant communities, and investigating ways to rebuild the prairie soils. A number of universities and nongovernmental organizations are involved in these efforts. The Tallgrass Prairie Center at the University of Northern Iowa, the Konza Prairie Biological Station at Kansas State University, and hundreds of other people, institutions, universities, agencies, and organizations are learning how to more closely replicate the original prairie sod and plant and animal communities. We are starting to think about restoring landscapes and landscape functions, not just an acre here and there.

One problem for prairie is the way many people perceive it. There are no stately mountains or thundering waterfalls. There are no majestic trees with great leafy limbs arching over our heads. It's just a bunch of grass, an unmown lawn. Some see native wildflowers as little more than weeds. But it was once a vast and magnificent ecosystem. There is grandeur there, but it's subtle. Quayle (1905) understood this when he said, "I think the prairie will die without finding a voice."

CHAPTER 3

The Lek

Anyone who has often heard the booming prairie chickens comes to associate the sound with its country. Somehow it symbolizes and partakes of the whole essence and flavor of open, uninhabited wild country. —*W. Grange 1948*

Someone wrote that the prairie chicken's booming was of great comfort to the pioneer. I can't imagine why. Many things can be said of the prairie chicken noise, but by no measure is it a comforting or civilized sound. It is a lonely wild sound made by a lonely wild bird. It has the quality of an ancient wind blowing across the smokeflap of the wickiup, companion noise to an Indian courting flute and the drum of unshod pony hooves on bluestem sod. In all of modern America, there is no more lost, plaintive, old-time sound than the booming of the native prairie chicken. —*Madson 1982*

Several times it was necessary to remind myself that it was only birds producing the dirge-like strains. It seemed more in keeping that it should be the wailing drone of a native ceremonial occasioned by some great tribal loss. —*H. Grange 1996*

Although called booming, their notes have the soft texture and smoothness of a mourning dove's notes and the melancholic aspect of some lost soul seeking forgiveness. —*Johnsgard 2003*

When we walk in the prairies, forests, or deserts, we often see ecological processes at work. We see plants flowering, bees pollinating, tracks in the mud, birds in the branches, deer in the field, half-chewed acorns, fur and blood droplets and the wing impressions of a hawk in the snow. From these signs we can tell an ecological story.

Evolution is harder to visualize. However, evolution and ecology are tightly linked. In 1965, G. Evelyn Hutchinson, one of the fathers of modern ecology, presented a series of lectures he titled "The Ecological Theater and Evolutionary Play." This title points out that evolution happens in the context of ecological processes, much as a play is performed inside a theater. It is ecological pressures that cause populations to evolve.

Evolution is both very simple and the most complex process in the universe. Simply, within a population there is variation in a trait or a number of traits. Some individuals will be taller, shorter, faster, slower, have stronger or weaker immune systems, and so forth. Individuals with certain traits will be better at passing those traits to the next generation than those without the traits. To be even more concise, whoever has the most kids wins.

Most people know the phrase "survival of the fittest." Fitness, as defined by ecologists, is the number of offspring an organism successfully raises. Each organism—animal, plant, fungus, or microbe—will have a different level of success at reproduction.

When observing nature, most people find it difficult to see or measure differences in reproductive success. With prairie-chickens and the other prairie grouse, competition and differences in reproduction are about as clear as they can be. When you watch a lek on an April morning, you are watching evolution happen. A female is selecting the male with the best traits and choosing him to pass both his and her genes on to the next generation. That's evolution!

Every spring a number of males gather in a small area and perform visual and auditory displays. The males are competing with each other for the attention of the females. Prairie-chickens have large orange sacs on the sides of their neck that they can inflate, as well as combs of bare orange skin above their eyes. They also erect their tail feathers, displaying bright white feathers on the underside. As the orange neck sacs expand and contract, the males emit a deep booming sound.

Waiting in the predawn prairie darkness for the morning to start can be an almost surreal experience.

The sound began before the sunrise, when the light was a violet paling over the stars. And it began out on the world's rim and was picked up, relayed, washed on, and boastfully flung back. It came to the sleeping grove and ringed the shagbarks and burr oaks round. There were booming surges of this sound that came in, first a crest and then a just discernible trough of silence, closed by another wave. (Peattie 1938)

At short range the bird's note suggested the mellow resonant tone of a kettledrum, and when bird after bird, all still unseen, uttered its truly startling call, the very earth echoed with a continuous roar. (Chapman 1908)

The booming of the prairie chicken is an unforgettable event. The sound has great resonance, a peculiar low rolling tone and is mystifyingly subtle. One hears it and starts out on foot to trace the sound to its source, which is apparently just over in the next meadow, but to his surprise finds that the booming has come to him across the cool, moist April-laden marshes for more than a mile. At close range the sound is not particularly loud so that one wonders how in the world it could have carried so far. (W. Grange 1948)

Each person who hears the prairie-chickens, up close or at a distance, seems to come away with a different description of the sounds of the lek.

This noise is a sort of ventriloquism. It does not strike the ear of the bystander with much force, but impresses him with the idea, though produced within a few rods of him, of a voice a mile or two distant. This note is highly characteristic. Though very peculiar, it is termed tooting, from its resemblance to the blowing of a conch or horn from a remote quarter. (Wilson 1839)

The males [were] strutting and erecting their plumage like a peacock, and uttering a long, loud, mournful note, something like the cooing of a dove, but resembling still more the sound produced by passing a rough finger over the surface of a tambourine. (Van Tramp 1868)

[The birds' sound was like] the lower notes of an ocarina or the sound made by blowing across the open neck of a bottle. (Schwartz 1945)

It was a soft note like the alto horn in the orchestra, a sweet do, re, mi of the chromatic scale which filled the still air of our mornings and evenings with harmony like nothing else I have ever heard. (Quick 1925)

The sound produced is not unlike the sound of a distant fog horn or a muffled tug-boat whistle. (Gross 1930)

As the quotes at the beginning of this chapter demonstrate, some people interpret the low-frequency notes of the prairie-chicken as dirge-like, lonely, lost, plaintive, or melancholic. However, other people interpret them differently. The booming of the prairie-chicken, especially in the northern prairies, was one of the first signs that the long, dark, cold winter was over and that the warmth of spring was on its way.

Once the snow had melted that spring they found dead horses and cattle and the bodies of several men and schoolchildren on the prairie near their homestead. But despite the heartbreak, Mary remembered that "Never was a spring more beautiful. The birds came back, the flowers bloomed, and the grouse and prairie chickens boomed and strutted on the knoll northwest of our house." (Laskin 2004)

Spring came to us that year with such a sudden beauty, such sweet significance after our long and depressing winter, that it seemed a release from prison, and when at the close of a warm day in March, we heard, pulsing down through the golden haze of sunset, the mellow boom, boom, boom of the prairie cock our hearts quickened, for this, we were told, was the certain sign of spring. (Garland 1917)

Once the sun crests the eastern horizon, all hell breaks loose. Although the following descriptions are evocative, the springtime mating rituals of the prairie-chicken truly need to be seen to be believed.

When the dawn is past, the ceremony begins by a low tooting from one of the cocks. This is answered by another. They then come forth one by one from the bushes, and strut about with all the pride and ostentation they can display. They seem to vie with each other in stateliness; and, as they pass each other, frequently cast looks of insult, and utter notes of defiance. These are the signals for battle. They engage with wonderful spirit and fierceness. During these contests, they leap a foot or two from the ground, and utter a cackling, screaming, and discordant cry. (Wilson 1839)

These prairie hen concerts were strange orgies of strutting and dancing. The cock would perform all sorts of antics, and then, erecting the beautiful cupid's wings above his neck, and swelling those odd skin pouches which grew near them into great balls like oranges, he would, with spread wings, take a half-dozen steps forward and with his neck outstretched emit his sonorous "Do, re, mi," to delight his companions and excite their emulation. (Quick 1925)

The display areas are generally called leks. However, "lek" is a generic term that can have several interpretations. A lek can be a place or location where males congregate, but it can also refer to the display behavior, or to the breeding system within a species. While the most famous lekking species are gallinaceous birds around the world, other species of birds, as well as some African deer and even many insects, lek (Hoglund and Alatalo 1995). Bradbury (1981) identified four criteria for lek mating systems. First, there is no male parental care. Second, there is a location where the males congregate and where most mating occurs. Third, this site has no resources the females need such as food or nest sites. Fourth, females visit the lek to choose their mate by comparing males side by side.

Perhaps the key feature of a lek is the concept of female mate choice, which leads to the phenomenon of sexual selection. All the males gather in one place, try to look tougher, bigger, better, and more flamboyant than the other males, and hope that the females choose them. If the idea of guys hanging out together and acting loud and obnoxious to try to impress the ladies sounds primitive to you, go to almost any bar on a Friday night.

In most bird species, females select the males. The most the males can do is try to get selected. This puts strong evolutionary pressure on the males to look better than the other males so that the females will choose them. This is why male bluebirds are so blue, cardinals are so red, and peacocks have those long tails. In the world of mammals, that's why male deer have antlers.

These bright colors and loud displays are called sexual selection, a term first used by Charles Darwin in 1871. The basic idea behind sexual selection is that males develop ridiculously large or bright ornaments or outrageous behaviors that have no function other than attracting females. Sexual selection also explains why only the males of each species have ornaments. Females aren't trying to attract males, so they don't need ornamentation. Everyone learns in grade school that females are brown and camouflaged so they can hide while on the nest. That's half the story. The other reason females are drab is that they don't need to be bright. Because they are selecting mates instead of trying to get selected, they don't need ornamentation.

Sexual selection can lead to runaway characteristics. If colorful feathers or loud songs attract females, then brighter feathers and louder songs will attract more females. Imagine a group of males in a particular area. There is genetic variation among these males; some are more colorful or louder than others. Presumably, those ornaments are advertising that they are more fit than the other males in the area. The females select the males with the most colorful feathers. In the next generation, all the males will inherit their father's brightly colored feathers. However, there is still genetic variation. Some of the sons will be colorful and some will be very colorful. Females will now choose the very colorful males over the colorful males. The next generation of males will then be very colorful. After hundreds or thousands of generations, male traits become very exaggerated.

Sexual selection can seem to run counter to natural selection. Indeed, there are very few survival benefits to having brightly colored feathers or making loud noises. The amount of energy those ornaments and behaviors require could probably be better used putting on fat to survive the winter. Those bright feathers and loud calls not only attract females, they also attract predators. Anyone who has observed prairie-chickens for any reasonable amount of time will have seen hawks, owls, or coyotes attack birds on the lek when they are too distracted to pay attention to their surroundings. However, without these ornaments or behaviors, no female would choose a male, and his genes would not survive into the next generation. The goal of evolution is to get the maximum number of your genes into the next generation. Each male has to find the evolutionary balance between keeping himself alive in the present and keeping his genes alive in the future.

The male is advertising several things with his ornaments or displays. He is saying, "I have such good genes and I'm so good at gathering resources that I have all this extra energy to spend being big or bright or loud. Those other guys with the small ornaments or dull feathers can barely get by and they have no extra energy to be big or flashy like me. If I can be the father of your children, they will get my good genes."

Hamilton and Zuk (1982) developed another, related theory. Wild animals are covered, inside and out, with parasites. (Think about how much money we spend on flea, tick, and worm medicines for our pets to keep them parasite free.) Parasites will make any animal weaker.

Big, bold, bright, loud displays by a male tell the female that he is better at fighting off parasites than his competitor is. The other males have to spend energy fighting parasites, and as a result their feathers are dull and drab. Since he has a strong immune system that is resistant to parasites, he can use that energy to be bright and loud. He is telling the females, "Pick me because I can resist parasites and I'll give your children a strong immune system."

In Kansas, Ballard and Robel (1974) found that on leks with an average of ten males, the two dominant males had 89 percent of the matings with females. Observers can literally sit and watch females choose a mate: sexual selection at work. The "sexiest" males tend to pass their genes on with female after female while the majority of the males don't pass on any genes at all. Why did these other eight males spend hours every day for several weeks displaying to attract females if they were rarely, if ever, able to mate? They put themselves at risk from predators and they took time away from gathering resources such as food, but they didn't get to pass any of their genes to the next generation. That's a lose-lose evolutionary situation.

Nooker and Sandercock (2008) presented some data that would not have been predicted. They found that there was no relationship between annual survival and male mating success or mating traits. If males have good genes and females allow the males to mate, it follows that those genes should increase survival. But that was not the case in this study. The researchers found that the size of the comb, the orange skin above the eyes, was the only morphological predictor of mating success. They did find that both display and aggressive behaviors were correlated with mating success, contrary to other studies in which such a correlation was not found.

Several theories explain why these other males hang out with the dominant males. If one of the dominant males disappears, a subordinate male may be able to slip into the spot as the new dominant male. Second is the idea of kin selection. If two males are brothers, they share many of the same genes since they both received all their genes from the same two parents. If the dominant brother mates, the subordinate brother does, indirectly, get some of his genes passed along to the next generation. Because bigger leks may attract more females, the subordinate male is actually both helping his brother mate with more females and indirectly helping his own genes.

With prairie-chickens, leks are more properly called booming grounds. The prairie-chickens' booming ground has several basic requirements. First, it must have short vegetation to maximize the males' visibility to females. Historically, these would have been burned areas, heavily grazed or trampled areas, places matted down by the winter's snow, or often hilltops where the grass grew shorter. Today, many booming grounds are located in hay fields or agricultural fields. Second, there should be some thick escape cover nearby as well as good nesting areas for the hens. Third, there should be few trees in the area. Trees provide perches for hawks that wouldn't mind a chicken breakfast.

In Missouri, Schwartz (1945) described three types of behavior on the booming grounds: territorial displays, booming, and mating. Territorial disputes on the booming grounds begin as early as January, or perhaps in the previous fall. During this time the males test each other to determine a dominance hierarchy. Schwartz (1945) found that booming grounds ranged in size from 50 by 50 square yards to 150 by 75 square yards. Horak (1985), working in Chase County, Kansas, found that individual territories on one booming ground ranged in size from 55 to 220 square yards.

Robel (1967) found that territories for dominant males ranged in size from 817 to 1,069 square meters (977 to 1,279 square yards). These dominant birds occupied the center of the lek. Peripheral males had territory sizes ranging from 192 to 655 square meters (230 to 783 square yards). Most researchers have stated that the dominant males with the largest territories occupy the center of the lek and are often the most aggressive. Nooker and Sandercock (2008) found, in contrast to previous studies, that territory size or position was not an important predictor of mating success. Their study was conducted in the same general area of Kansas where Robel worked.

One function of a dominant male or males is to maintain some form of social order within the lek. Basically, no one wants to start a fight with the dominant birds. Ballard and Robel (1974) removed the dominant birds from several leks and found that without the stabilizing influence of the dominant males, the fighting among the peripheral males increased dramatically as they fought to establish their own dominance. More importantly, as the males fought, their reproductive success declined. Before removal, the dominant males had a successful copulation rate of 92 percent. However, after the dominant males were removed, copulation success dropped to 13 percent.

Most of the displays are bluffs, in which males try to intimidate each other but rarely risk a fight. There are three possible results of fighting. The dominant male could win, he could win but be injured, or he could lose. It's best to avoid fights whenever possible and just try to look tougher than the other guy. Nobody gets hurt when bluffing. Rarely is there actual combat, but when it happens, feathers fly.

But this was the opening gesture of a combat dance. Now male pride erected the stiff tail brush while the excited white feathers showed like the cottontail's scut or the snowy hairs on the deer's rump. And male rage lowered the bird's head, where the neck tufts shot up, black and white and conspicuous as a second tail. Between this gorgeous featherwork the throat sacs bulged like painted war drums, crowing the retorts to all other males who had the insolence to live. The tympanum resonated till the furious whoop ran rippling with the greater, the composite wave, towards the shores of dawn. He whirled around as he leaped, and came down crest to crest with the second bird, who leaped and met his rival at halfway. They whirled about like fencers, backed, and boomed, ran in too close and became a blur. Out of the first swift passage both emerged to boom again, leaving a drift of feathers on the grass. (Peattie 1938)

The activity on the booming ground peaks in mid-April. This is the middle of the roughly six-week window from late March to early May when females visit the booming grounds and mating occurs. Birds will start earlier in March in Kansas and go longer into May in Minnesota.

Activity varies over the course of the morning. Males begin displaying approximately thirty minutes before sunrise. Peak activity is at sunrise. Activity then decreases over the rest of the morning and generally stops about ninety minutes after sunrise.

It's easy to tell when a female appears at the booming ground. She will usually fly in, land at some distance, and then walk to the edge. While the booming was steady before, once a female appears the cackling becomes quite loud. The female examines the males, sometimes over several mornings. Once she decides, she proceeds to the male, squats, allows the male to mount her, and she is gone. It takes only a second.

CHAPTER 4

Hens, Nests, and Chicks

There are records from 1845 to 1869 showing that farmers burned the prairies in the spring just before plowing and sometimes deliberately to kill birds which would later feed on the grain so that thousands of scorched eggs could be found in the fields alongside the bodies of young birds. —*Scott 1947*

It was a common practice with farmers to burn off the prairies in the spring to remove the dead top grass. Unfortunately, this was habitually done when the prairies were covered with nests of the prairie chicken, and untold numbers of nests and even young were mercilessly destroyed in this way. After the fires had passed over these tracts, eggs were gathered up by the bushel. —*Pierce 1922*

While making the Game Survey of Iowa old-timers repeatedly described to me the great concentrations of prairie chicken nests which followed the prairie fires of pioneer days. Several said one could not walk across the unburned patches of grass without crushing chicken eggs at every step. —*Leopold 1933*

I remember once on a Sunday morning in spring, after a prairie fire, going with my brother hunting prairie chickens' eggs. In that morning stroll my brother and I found about two hundred eggs, some of them slightly cooked, but most of them ready for boiling for our dinners. —*Quick 1925*

Schwartz (1945) describes the hen's nest as a simple, flimsily built structure constructed of dead grass, seven inches in diameter and two to three inches deep. These nests once occurred at very high densities on the prairie.

> The farmers in northwestern Illinois, in the early seventies, burned the prairies in the spring after nesting had started and afterwards gathered large numbers of eggs for household use. (Schorger 1944)

Losing a nest to a fire, especially early in the season, isn't the end of the story. Prairie-chickens and most other grassland-nesting birds will renest after a nest has been destroyed by fire, flood, or predator. Second nests do usually have lower numbers of eggs, probably because of the physiological cost to the hen of the original clutch of eggs. They simply don't have enough energy left over to produce another full clutch. Some have speculated that second nest attempts of game birds are more successful because the chicks will hatch later in the summer when there is more food—that is, insects—available.

The hen lays, on average, a dozen eggs. One egg is laid every one and a half to two days. The first eggs laid are held in suspended animation until the last egg is laid and the hen starts to incubate the entire clutch, which she will do for twenty-four to twenty-five days. The larger ground-nesting birds—grouse, pheasants, ducks, and geese—must begin incubating their eggs all at the same time, so that they all hatch at the same time. If the hen were to incubate the eggs as she laid them, the chicks would hatch over a two-week period. The first chicks would have to stay around the nest waiting for their siblings to hatch. This would be very dangerous, as they would be vulnerable to predators.

Prairie-chicken chicks are precocial; they are born with a full complement of fluffy feathers. While they will not be able to fly for a few weeks, they are able to run and walk and are able to leave the nest within hours of hatching. Chicks on the move are less vulnerable than they would be if they stayed around a central location like a nest.

Many tree-nesting birds such as songbirds, hawks, and owls produce altricial young. These birds are blind and naked when they emerge from the shells and are almost helpless. However, because they live in the safety of a well-protected nest, they can take the time to grow feathers and become mobile. Grassland songbirds use this same strategy but are much more vulnerable. Some of these birds incubate the eggs as they are laid. By the time the bird in the last egg hatches, its siblings may be several days old and significantly larger. This can lead to some bullying in the nest and, if food becomes scarce, to cannibalism of the youngest by the oldest.

Gross (1930) found that the average prairie-chicken hen in Wisconsin weighed 734 grams, or one and a half to two pounds. The eggs weigh, on average, 21 grams, and collectively they weigh 252 grams. That's 34 percent of the weight of the hen. To put that in perspective, it would be the equivalent of a 125-pound woman giving birth to a 43-pound baby! Or put another way, that's the equivalent of the same woman giving birth to a 3.6-pound baby. While that baby would be considered a premature birth weight, the woman would produce another baby in two days. And another and another.

In mammals, the development of the baby takes place inside the mother. In birds, the development takes place after the egg is laid. However, the hen is still producing that much mass every day or two. In essence, it takes humans nine months to produce the weight of a baby. It takes a hen one to two days, and she does it twelve times in a row. Imagine how much stress that puts on her body. That's also a lot of food she has to eat. More specifically, that's a lot of protein to eat. For almost all birds, protein means insects. One study found that a wood duck hen, roughly the same size as a prairie-chicken, has to eat thirty thousand insects and other invertebrates to gain enough protein to lay a clutch of eggs.

The prairie lover in me wants to say that prairie-chickens need native prairie or at least prairie grasses for nesting.

The higher population densities in Missouri are associated with the remaining native tallgrass prairies. (Christisen 1981)

However, there are some reports in the literature that contradict that idea.

> This quantity of grassland appears especially workable if brome (*Bromus inermis*), a preferred grass, is emphasized in sanctuary management. (Westemeier 1997)

> There is no evidence that greater prairie chickens prefer native grasses or that natives create better nesting habitat. (Toepfer 2003)

Svedarsky (1988) found twice as many nests in bluestem as in brome. However, nesting success was higher in the brome. In Nebraska, Matthews et al. (2013) found more nests and higher nest success in Conservation Reserve Program fields planted to both warm-season and cool-season grasses relative to adjacent rangelands.

Kirsch (1974) cited four different studies and lists Kentucky bluegrass, redtop, timothy, quackgrass, sweet clover, and brome as nesting habitat. Christisen (1981), after making the noted quoted statement, went on to say that prairie-chickens lingered in a habitat containing Kentucky bluegrass, redtop, and timothy. None of these are native grasses. W. Grange (1948) listed six species of grass used by prairie-chickens, the four mentioned plus bluejoint grass and cordgrass, which are native species. In Wisconsin, prairie-chickens preferred to nest in quack grass, Kentucky bluegrass, and reed canary grass. F. N. Hamerstrom (1939) found most nests in Kentucky bluegrass. Schwartz (1945) found fifty-seven nests. Six of these were in native bluestem, and the rest were in timothy, redtop, bluegrass, crabgrass, barnyard grass, ragweed, and sweet clover. The more difficult question is whether the hens preferred these nonnative grasses or whether these grasses were all that remained to nest in because there was no native prairie left on the landscape.

Yeatter (1943) states that the only reason prairie-chickens survived in Illinois is the redtop grass seed industry and the nesting cover this type of grass provided. Most nests were found in fields of Kentucky bluegrass, timothy, or redtop.

> The bluegrass fields of Buena Vista [Wisconsin] seemed to be the chicken's salvation, but competition from other regions put the seed

people out of business, and the prairie chicken faced extinction. (Laycock 1963)

Grass seed harvest provides a couple of benefits to all grassland-nesting birds, not just prairie-chickens. First, seed harvest doesn't start until mid to late summer, so there is no disruption of the nest while the hen is incubating eggs. When farmers and ranchers cut grass for hay, they cut the grass as low as possible to get the maximum amount of hay from each acre. This leaves little residual cover for nesting the following spring. When seed is harvested, the grasses are cut above the tops of the leaves so that only the seedheads are gathered. This leaves abundant cover for nesting the following spring. Is it the species of grass or the management of the grass that the birds are focusing on?

Westemeier and Edwards (1987) stated that nesting cover should be around sixteen inches or lower. Christisen (1981) stated that most nests were in cover eight to fifteen inches tall. Horak (1985) found nests in stubble twelve inches tall in Kansas. Blus and Walker (1966) found similar results in Nebraska, as did Svedarsky (1988) and Syrowitz (2013) in Minnesota.

The previous summer's growth from native grasses may be higher than this, unless a snowy winter mats down the grasses. The tall, dense stands of native big bluestem, often used in the Conservation Reserve Program and similar habitat restoration programs, may provide habitat that is taller and thicker than what prairie-chickens prefer. Exotic cool-season grasses, like those listed, may create a structure more suitable to nesting, and the hens may actually prefer these areas over some areas with restored native grasses. Or, light grazing of these fields of dense bluestem may create a structure more suitable for prairie-chicken nests.

The structure versus species question is interesting, as several questions are actually involved. The first is regarding plant diversity. Often, introduced grasses are planted in monoculture, while some native grass plantings have wildflowers mixed in. Maximum diversity is usually reached with native prairie that has never seen a plow. Birds may or may not care how many plant species are present. More plants with different shapes and sizes may create more structural heterogeneity in the grass for the birds to choose from when deciding exactly where to build their nest or forage later in the summer.

The second question is the height of the grass itself. One of my colleagues said it most succinctly: if you want to find pheasants, walk through waist-high grass; if you want to find prairie-chickens, walk through knee-high grass. Another friend hypothesized that this has to do with the escape behavior of pheasants and prairie-chickens. When scared, pheasants like to run and dart into the thickest cover they can find. Tall, thick grasses or cattails are perfect for this. Prairie-chickens like to fly to escape danger. It's difficult for them to get off the ground when they have to fight through four feet of grass stems.

The last question deals with the physiology of the grasses. Most introduced grasses are cool-season grasses, while the majority of native grasses are warm-season grasses. This simply refers to the way the grasses conduct photosynthesis. Cool-season grasses green up as soon as possible in the spring and are growing vigorously by the nesting season. Warm-season grasses don't start growing until late spring. Do birds find better concealment in actively growing grasses? Or do they find more insects to feed on in the green introduced grasses than in the still-brown native grasses?

As is typical with most grassland-nesting birds, prairie-chicken nest success is low. In eight different studies in Wisconsin, a combined average of 50.8 percent of nests successfully hatched chicks. In Minnesota, nest success ranged from 33.1 percent in young cool-season Conservation Reserve Program fields to 47.6 percent in older fields to 55 percent in native prairie. Nest success in South Dakota and North Dakota was 66 percent and 58 percent, respectively. All of these studies sampled a relatively low number of nests. Finding and monitoring nests takes an incredible amount of time. Depending on the species you are looking for, you could go a day or two between finding nests. This makes nesting studies difficult, time consuming, and expensive.

One emerging threat to nest success is nest parasitism by pheasant hens. Hen pheasants find prairie-chicken nests and lay one to several eggs in them. This is a good strategy for the pheasant: the hen can produce many new chicks for the next generation but never incubates any of them. Pheasants are just one of many bird species that nest-dump into another nest. Some species parasitize nests of other females of the same species, some parasitize those of other species, and some opportunistically parasitize any nest they can find. Cowbirds are probably the best-known nest parasite of songbirds.

Pheasant eggs need to incubate for only twenty-one to twenty-three days before hatching. Prairie-chicken eggs need to incubate about two days longer. When the pheasant egg or eggs hatch, the prairie-chicken hen is genetically programmed to leave the area with her chicks immediately. The problem is that these aren't her chicks. The bigger problem is that all her eggs are now abandoned two or three days before they should hatch, and all of them will die.

Once off the nest, those tiny chicks can cover a lot of ground. Svedarsky (1988) found that hens had a home range of 200 acres before egg laying, 77 acres during the laying period, and from 24 to 78 acres when they had a brood of chicks with them.

The diet of the prairie-chicken varies by age, season, and location. During the first few weeks of life, almost 100 percent of the diet is insects. A newly hatched chick weighs about 15 grams, or 0.03 pound, but it will weigh almost 2 pounds by the fall. That means that over the course of the summer, it must increase its weight 67 times from May to October. An equivalent weight gain for humans would mean that a 7.5-pound baby would weigh 503 pounds at its six-month checkup!

As the birds mature, they move to a more vegetarian diet. During the fall they eat fruits and grains. During the winter, they spend much of their time foraging for waste grain in farm fields. Several researchers have listed the diets of prairie-chickens, throughout the year and by season (see Korschgen 1962 for a review). To summarize, prairie-chickens eat everything: insects, leaves, fruits, and seeds.

CHAPTER 5

Original Range and Expansion

The prairie chicken was common in regions practically
untouched by agriculture. —*Schorger 1944*

As the Illinois timberlands were cleared and put under the plow, prairie
chickens extended their range into these areas from the adjacent
prairies, in which the first settlers had found them. —*Yeatter 1943*

After settlement of the country began, I am certain that for a
while they increased rapidly in numbers. They still had ample
areas of nesting ground, and the fields of the new farmers
gave them an increased supply in food. —*Quick 1925*

The pinnated grouse followed the clearings into the forest, as they
became large enough to offer suitable range. —*Leopold 1931*

Midwestern vegetation and habitats changed very quickly during
the 1800s, and prairie-chickens responded just as fast. With settlement, fires became much less common, leading to a rapid expansion
of forests. "Whenever the dominion of man is sufficiently established
in these vast plains, to prevent the annual ravages of fire, trees will
spring up" (James 1819). People were noting changes in land cover,
mostly the forestation of grasslands, within just a few years of the
Lewis and Clark Expedition. At the same time, settlers were cutting
down forests to make towns and cornfields.

There is controversy about the density of birds in the presettlement Midwest. Some argue that prairie-chickens existed at relatively

low densities, but other authorities question this. There are some reports of dense populations from presettlement times.

> The prairies were but sparsely settled and not an acre in a thousand had been broken up. The grouse were in immense numbers. (Bogardus 1878)

> The prairie hen was found in great abundance by the first settlers of Michigan. (Watkins 1901, quoted in Ammann 1957)

Featherstonhaugh (1847) reported from his tour of the Minnesota River in 1835 that "grouse were abundant, and rose booming and screaming in every direction." In other places the prairies were "abounding in grouse." In still other places he described the prairies as "being literally alive with *Tetrao*." However, some of these may have been sharp-tailed grouse, as described earlier.

Many reports state that prairie-chickens weren't in much of the presettlement prairie, especially the western parts of the ecosystem, and that the birds followed the plow in these areas.

> In 1882, when I first visited Manitoba, the species was nearly unknown in the country, the only known specimens having been taken near Winnipeg in 1881. In 1883, Mr. Hine informs me, it began to be common at Pembina. (Seton 1891)

> The chicken follows the plow, which accounts for the gradual extension of its range westward. (Sandys and Van Dyke 1924)

> After 1866 he moved to Iowa and again the chickens moved in when he grubbed out a farm. (Beck 1957)

> They flourished with early farming. (Madson 1982)

In Iowa, prairie-chickens were once found statewide wherever there was suitable grassland habitat. Although they were common at the time of settlement, there is evidence that prairie-chicken numbers increased over much of the state after settlement, especially in the nonwooded sections. (Dinsmore 1994)

These early years created ideal habitat for the prairie-chicken. Some of the land was broken and planted to crops. The waste grain in these fields provided abundant food. At the same time, there was still a large amount of nesting cover in the remaining prairies, pastures, and hay fields. The birds seemed to do the best when the landscape was about 50 percent grass and 50 percent crops.

At the same time the chickens were following the plow into the prairies, they were following the ax and saw into the forests.

Figure 1. Estimated original, or presettlement, range of the prairie-chicken. Light gray: Johnsgard (2002); dark gray: Baker (1953).

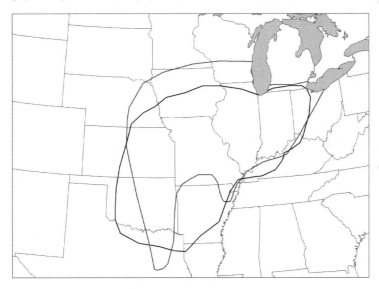

Chickens of both species arrived about 1919, and by 1925 there was a high year during which the chickens were exceedingly abundant [in Pine County, Wisconsin]. (Leopold 1931)

It is unlikely that there were any prairie chickens native to the Upper Peninsula before the arrival of the white man. In the early 1900s prairie chickens found their way into the Upper Peninsula, presumably from Wisconsin, following the conquest of the northern forests by man with ax, fire, and plow. (Ammann 1957)

My grandfather settled at Marietta Ohio and grubbed farm land out of the big tree country of the Northwest Territories in 1833. He said the prairie chicken moved in. (Beck 1957)

Several people have tried to plot the original, presettlement range of the prairie-chicken. While they all generally agree, the edges are different on each map (fig. 1).

We do know that prairie-chickens expanded their range quickly (fig. 2). Probably one of the best-documented cases of the expansion of prairie-chickens comes from Minnesota, North Dakota, and the Prairie Provinces of Canada. Some reports (Baker 1953) state that the prairie-chicken did not originally occur in Minnesota. If it did, it would have been in only the southern tier of counties (Leopold 1931). In contrast, Schorger (1944) placed the presettlement range of Wisconsin prairie-chickens as far north as Minneapolis and Saint Paul. Featherstonhaugh (1847) described "heavy grouse" in west-central Minnesota in the 1830s. If these were prairie-chickens and not sharp-tailed grouse, this would extend the species' presettlement range significantly to the northwest. These discrepancies are reflected in figure 1. Unfortunately, we didn't have biologists running around in the late 1700s mapping where each species was.

We do know that birds were reported from the Fort Snelling (Saint Paul, Minnesota) area in 1839. They reached Fargo, North Dakota, around 1879 and Winnipeg, Manitoba, in 1881 (Partch 1970). This means they moved northward at a rate of about 9.4 miles per

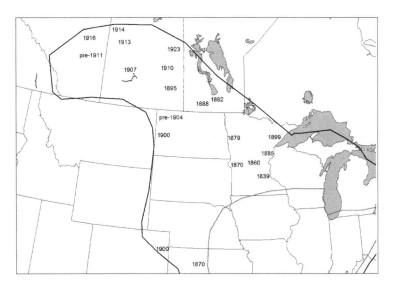

Figure 2. Range expansion of prairie-chickens to the north and west. Data from numerous sources.

year over that period. By 1916 prairie-chickens were seen in Bawlf, Alberta. The birds moved across North Dakota at a rate of 16 miles per year and arrived in eastern Montana around 1900. Prairie-chickens moved into Colorado from Kansas in approximately 1899 (Baker 1953). Thus, they expanded to the west at a rate of just under 20 miles per year.

To the east and north, prairie-chickens were seen on the North Shore of Lake Superior by 1900. There are reports of prairie chickens near Ely, Minnesota. When we think of far northeastern Minnesota we picture moose, wolves, and loons. But we don't think of prairie-chickens. At different times they covered all of northern Wisconsin, northern Michigan, and Michigan's Upper Peninsula.

We know today that prairie-chickens are relatively intolerant of trees. This just illustrates how profoundly Americans altered the northern pineries during the 1800s, turning towering forests of white pine and other trees into open landscapes suitable for a bird whose name starts with "prairie."

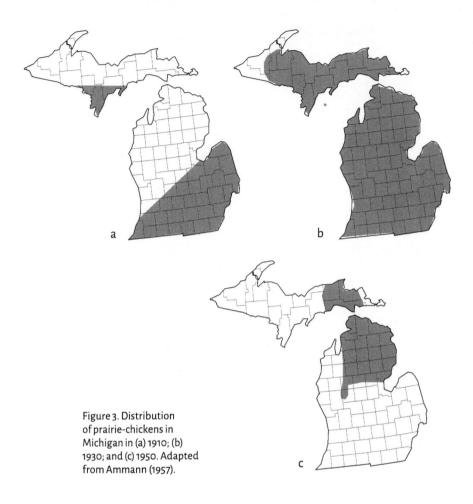

Figure 3. Distribution of prairie-chickens in Michigan in (a) 1910; (b) 1930; and (c) 1950. Adapted from Ammann (1957).

The maps of Michigan shown in figure 3 illustrate that it's irrelevant to ask what the range of the prairie-chicken is in that state. The only way to ask the question is to qualify it with a date, as in where were chickens in Michigan in 1940? The same basic idea could be applied to the entire chicken range, from western Ohio to eastern Colorado. There was probably never a time when the birds occupied the entire range. By the time they were pioneering into the western edges of their range, they were disappearing on the eastern side.

The other factor in this expansion is the change in abundance. This simply shows the reproductive abilities of the prairie-chicken. As a general rule, wildlife populations are at low densities along the edges of a species' range and at higher densities in the center of the range. As that range shifts, so do areas where the species is abundant.

In many cases, prairie-chicken populations grew so much that they became problems for farmers. Prairie-chickens are decent-sized birds. Seeing a flock of several hundred descend on the winter's stored grain would probably be worrisome to any farmer relying on that grain to pay the mortgage and feed the livestock. In many areas, prairie-chickens were blamed for significant crop damage during the winter months.

> They perpetuated quite as much mischief upon the tender buds and fruits of the orchards, as well as the grain in the fields, and were often so destructive to the crops that it was absolutely necessary for the farmers to employ their young negroes to drive them away. (Lewis 1863)

> It was no uncommon thing to see whole cornfields overrun and ruined by them in the 60s. Prairie chickens sat down in the cornfield and ruined it much as the barbarians crowded around a fortified city for plunder. (Merritt 1904)

> Most of the ears are nothin' but bare cobs. Them cussed prairie hens have picked all the corn off. (Quick 1925)

> The country hereabouts is full of them. Pesky things are eating the farmers out of house and home. (Betten 1940)

> Usually during the first few years of settlement, it increases rapidly, and is often a nuisance to the pioneer farmers. (Webb, quoted in M. Johnson and Knue 1989)

Dear me, what a pest they were for several years, for they destroyed cornfields rapidly. (Tasker, quoted in Greenberg 2002)

However, at other times prairie-chickens were seen as saving the farmers from plagues of insects in their crop fields.

The grasshoppers eaten by a single prairie-chicken would be sufficient in number to destroy several bushels of grain. (quoted in Swanson 2007)

The birds are too valuable as grasshopper exterminators to allow their wholesale destruction by city sportsmen. (quoted in Swanson 2007)

Expansions in the range of wildlife species are easy to note and document. The prairie-chicken is a relatively large bird, and it's hard to believe that it could have gone unnoticed by farmers and settlers who spent every daylight hour outside. They would have been seen and noted as soon as they arrived in any particular area.

Monitoring the contraction of a species' range is much harder. If a bird went from abundant to extinct overnight, we would note it. But that's generally not how it happens. The species goes from abundant to common to uncommon to rare. The population slowly and gradually fades away.

Its virgin prairie habitat broken and destroyed, the prairie chicken faded away from most of its range as quietly as a moccasined footstep. (Madson 1962)

Eventually someone says something like, "They aren't as common as they used to be." This is followed by, "I haven't seen any around here for a few years." It's hard to put an exact date to that type of information.

While there are some smaller populations in Illinois, Wisconsin, and Missouri, today the largest populations of prairie-chickens are mostly outside and to the west of their original historic range (fig. 4).

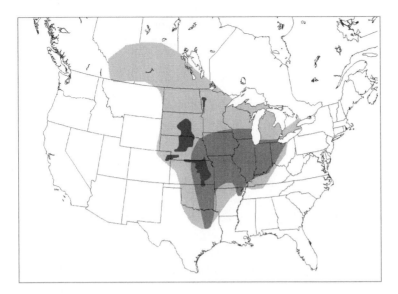

Figure 4. Prairie-chicken ranges: maximum range in light gray, original range in gray, and current range of largest populations in dark gray. Adapted from Svedarsky et al. (2000).

Minnesota is a good microcosm of prairie-chicken history. Before settlement, prairie-chickens were in only the southeastern corner, but they followed the plow westward and the ax northward until they occupied 92 percent of the state. As the forests regenerated and more grass was lost to the plow, the prairie-chicken population fragmented and contracted. Today, prairie-chickens are found in only seven or eight counties in the northwest part of the state, and at densities much lower than those of historic reports. Range maps for prairie-chickens in Minnesota in the late 1700s, late 1800s, and late 1900s would be completely different from each other. Today, prairie-chickens are in the opposite corner of the state from where they originally occurred.

There are numerous records of how abundant they were at different times in different parts of the state. In 1925, hunters shot 412,000 prairie-chickens in Minnesota as a whole (Svedarsky, Wolfe, and Toepfer 1999).

Prairie chickens were seen, sometimes in large numbers, sailing away from the tracks as the train dashed by. (W. T. D. 1887, quoted in Duebbert 2003)

There is a continuum from low density in the restricted area of the southeast, to abundance across the state, to low density in a totally different restricted area, the northwest.

Over this period, the density and abundance of the birds varied dramatically in space and time. There is no one time when we can say the Minnesota population peaked. Each area of the state probably peaked at a different time or times.

What is natural? What is desirable? Some would argue that maximum abundance is what we should manage for. However, that time of maximum abundance for prairie-chickens was a very unnatural period in the state's history. The landscape was heavily altered at that time by unsustainable logging practices. While prairie-chickens flourished then, we can imagine that many forest species were not doing as well.

Should we really make a goal of establishing prairie-chickens on the North Shore of Lake Superior? To do that, we would have to devastate the northern forests, again, and remove or alter the habitats of dozens of forest and shrubland species. This is a somewhat extreme example of the decisions wildlife managers make every day. Every action will affect some species more than others. Actions that benefit some species may be detrimental to other species.

CHAPTER 6

Harvest

It is decidedly the finest gallinaceous game, if it may so be called, of America, and affords the greatest sport to those who are so fortunate as to reside where it abounds. —*Forester 1866*

Of all the grouse family, this bird—the "chicken" of shooting lore—probably yields the most complete satisfaction to the great army of American sportsmen. For unquestionably it is the bird of the people. —*Sandys and Van Dyke 1924*

As much as I like hunting pheasants, I'd opt for chickens if I had the choice, both for the nature of the birds and for the aesthetic values of where they live. —*McIntosh 1997*

We had no reason for not killing as many prairie chickens as we could, so in winter we trapped them by the thousands. —*Quick 1925*

The prairie-chicken may be the only game bird in America that was not only extensively harvested with the gun but also extensively trapped. While quail and other game birds were trapped, this probably didn't happen at the same scale as prairie-chicken trapping. Trapping usually occurred in the winter when snow covered the fields and birds could easily be attracted to bait left on top of the snow. It's hard to guess whether trapping or shooting removed more birds from the landscape. While a shotgun harvested one bird at a time, a trap could capture dozens.

At first, birds were trapped as they came into barnyards, and we can assume that only a few were caught at any one time.

They were trapped in the barnyard, tolled under the traps by domestic fowls. (Askins 1931)

They used to come around farm buildings in the early morning; the farmer could often shoot them off his barn roofs with very little difficulty. (Pierce 1922)

Prairie hens (pinnated grouse) and quail come about the fences in hundreds, and with a very primitive trap, made of split sticks, with a figure 4 trigger, we caught numbers of both within view of the door of the house. (Oliver 1843)

During inclement weather, more birds were caught, as their wild foods were buried under the snow.

The number of birds killed by the gun was small in comparison to the many thousands taken by trapping. When snow covered the ground, they came into the barnyards to feed with the domestic fowls and were taken easily. (Schorger 1944)

The people of the Barrens informed me, that, when the weather becomes severe, with snow, they approach the barn and farm-house, are sometimes seen sitting on the fences in dozens, mix with the poultry, and glean up the scattered grains of Indian corn, seeming almost half domesticated. At such times, great numbers are taken in traps. (Wilson 1839)

Eventually, prairie-chicken trapping grew in scale.

Trapping is done almost entirely by farmers and destroys more game than all the market hunters, game hogs, and others combined. In my own trips in the latter part of the season I have never failed to see dozens of traps in plain sight from the wagon-roads. (W. R. H. 1894)

Trapping prairie chickens in Iowa seems to reach the zenith some time in the [eighteen] seventies. Every one in the country was apparently interested in trapping and marketing these birds. The trapping industry was current gossip everywhere. Well, how many "chickens" did you get today? was the stock question. (Pierce 1922)

Another family trapped 500 in a little over a week, in traps set in the garden. (Lockart 1960)

In 1894, a writer in western Iowa complained that dozens of traps could be seen along the roads near Owana. . . . Many people have spare time during the winter, and prairie-chickens provided a supplement to their diet and an extra cash crop from their land. (Dinsmore 1994)

We can imagine farm families on the winter prairies eating prairie-chickens for meal after meal.

When living in Dickey County [North Dakota] during the years 1885–94 we actually tired of eating prairie chickens. (quoted in M. Johnson and Knue 1989)

Farmers have always worked with a thin profit margin. Trapping birds provided an income during the winter months, when prairie-chickens were shipped eastward by the trainload. Westemeier (1985) cites reports from Illinois of prairie-chicken shipments measured by the cord and ton. Three hundred thousand prairie-chickens were shipped out of eastern and southeastern Nebraska in 1874 (Harrison 1974). Prairie-chickens were commonly seen hanging in butcher shops in most of the major eastern cities. In the 1870s, prairie-chickens made it even to the markets in Paris and London (M. Johnson and Knue 1989).

[From 1896] over two thousand North Dakota grouse had been seized by the Minnesota Game and Fish Commission in St Paul in early February. Mr. Wilder's informants in the Minnesota Department stated that none of the birds was carrying shot. They believed all had been trapped, removed from the traps, and their necks broken. (M. Johnson and Knue 1989)

A Mr. Reese of Bourbon County, trapped 920 prairie chickens in five days. He ought to be caught in the jaws of a powerful steel trap, and kept the remainder of his life. (*Ellsworth* [KS] *Reporter*, February 11, 1875, quoted in Fleharty 1995)

[In 1896] 25,000 prairie chickens were shipped to market from the village of Spooner alone. (Leopold 1949)

The hunting stories for this species seem almost ridiculous today. If there weren't so much evidence to support these numbers, they could easily be dismissed. Even if we acknowledge that hunters are occasionally apt to exaggerate just a bit, these numbers are stunning.

As recently as 1910 in northeastern Colorado, hunting camps were established on the Republican and South Platte Rivers, with wagons standing by to receive the daily kill. When each wagon left camp for market, its box, four feet wide and fifteen feet long, was heaped high with prairie chickens. (Dalrymple 1950)

The roar that followed my shot, occasioned by the beating of innumerable wings, was astonishing. So large were these flocks that came together at times in late Autumn and early Winter that their sudden and simultaneous rising would make the earth tremble beneath the shooter's feet. ("Prairie Chicken Shooting" 1883)

It was no feat then to kill a hundred head a day to each gun, and when, as it sometimes occurred, that a hundred or more were slaughtered to satisfy some citizen ambitious to boast at home of bag, the game could seldom all be given away, but had, in warm weather, be fed to the hogs. (Lowther 1883)

We went into it early in the morning, and came out about eleven o'clock in the forenoon with eighty full grown grouse. (Bogardus 1878)

The counties best shooter bagged 157 in a day with 152 shots. Still another note tells of four hunters who left Independence at 3:00 pm one day, drove fifteen miles and returned the next evening with 337 prairie chickens. (Pierce 1922)

In the period of plenty it was a daily event throughout the hunting season to meet parties of hunters returning from the field with all available space in their double buggies or light wagons packed full of prairie chickens; at the railway station were to be seen large heaps of hay-stuffed birds ready for shipment. (C. Johnson 1934)

In 1875, four hunters killed 153 prairie chickens at York Prairie. (Leopold 1949)

In Iowa, three men killed 410 prairie chickens in one hour on one 80 acre field. (Harrison 1974)

Capt Bogardus killed 600 prairie chickens in 10 days hunting only mornings and evenings. (Westemeier 1985)

Bird hunters and bird watchers today can only shake their heads in wonder at these numbers and descriptions. There is an important result of all this carnage, though: Leopold (1933) reported that the first bag limit, twenty-five prairie-chickens per day, was instituted in Iowa in 1878.

CHAPTER 7

Population Ups and Downs

The number of these fowls is astonishing. The plain is covered with them; and when they have been driven from the ground by deep snow, I have seen thousands—or more probably tens of thousands—thickly clustered in the tops of the trees surrounding the prairies. —*Hall, quoted in Plumbe 1839*

We saw great flights of prairie hens, or grouse, that hovered from tree to tree, or sat in rows along the naked branches, waiting until the sun should melt the frost from the weeds and herbage. —*Irving 1956*

Given proper environment, the prairie chicken has a reproductive rate sufficiently high to cope with predators, disease, accidents, and other hazards. —*Yeatter 1943*

Life for newly hatched prairie-chickens must be scary. They weigh practically nothing, are lost in a sea of grass, and have to spend every moment eating enough to survive, avoid predators and bad weather, and stay dry and warm. Mornings start with a cold dew on the grass, midday can be blazing hot, and then there are those late afternoon thunderstorms midwesterners know so well.

Applying numbers to the population ecology of prairie-chickens shows just how rough life is on the prairies. About half of the nests hatch eggs. In many waterfowl studies, nest success is often near or sometimes below 10 or 20 percent. McNew et al. (2012) found that nest survival in Kansas ranged from 4 to 28 percent. The average clutch of a prairie-chicken is roughly a dozen eggs. Brood sizes during the middle of the summer averaged 3.5 chicks in Wisconsin, 4.8 in Minnesota, and 4.9 in North Dakota (Hamerstrom 1939). McNew et al. (2012) found that only 27 to 34 percent of chicks survived to twenty-four days old.

After they reach adulthood, life doesn't get any better. Hamerstrom and Hamerstrom (1973) developed life tables for prairie-chickens. A life table simply follows a number of individuals from birth to death and determines how many survive at each stage, or year, of life. In human terms we would call this an actuarial table. They observed a total of 398 males that they placed leg bands on as immature (first-year) birds. Only 194 (49 percent) made it to their first birthday. Only 25 percent made it to their second year. Sixteen and 8 percent made it to years three and four, respectively. One male survived eight years.

To summarize, more than 50 percent of nests are lost. Of those chicks that hatch, half die by midsummer. Of those that survive to the first fall, only 50 percent survive to the following year. Only half of those survive until year two. Life is brutal.

From a management and conservation perspective, we need to understand what factors are most important in determining how populations grow or change. Populations are usually defined for a specific area—the mallard population in the prairie pothole region of the Upper Midwest or the pheasant population of Iowa, for example. Ideally, we define populations along biological boundaries (the prairie pothole region), but more often we define them along political boundaries (the state of Iowa). While birds don't recognize political boundaries, administrators and managers do.

The math behind population growth is easy. The population next year, or year two (N_{year2}), is determined by the number of individuals this year, or year one (N_{year1}), plus the number of births minus the number of deaths. We can add those that move into the population from adjacent areas (immigrants) and subtract those that move out of the area (emigrants). We can create an equation that looks like this:

$$N_{year2} = N_{year1} + \text{births} - \text{deaths} + \text{move in} - \text{move out}$$

That's easy. But determining the biological factors behind each of these four variables is mind-numbingly complex.

When it comes to studying populations, females are what matter. Scientists and managers want to know what is going to happen to the population, next year and into the future. In other words, how many young will be born? To answer this question, they need to know how many healthy females there are of reproductive age.

Let's say there are ten females in an imaginary population and each female can produce two offspring. It doesn't matter if there is one male with a harem of ten females, ten males each paired with a female, or one hundred (mostly frustrated) males. There will still be only twenty young born next year. This is why hunters can harvest pheasant roosters and white-tailed bucks, both males, without significantly harming the number of chicks or fawns born the following spring. The number of males is often irrelevant; the number of females is critical.

A number of factors can affect each of the four variables in this equation, all of which fall under the term "population regulation." Imagine an unregulated prairie-chicken population with no controls on its growth. Start with 5 males and 5 females. Each female lays twelve eggs each year, and half of those are daughters. If we assume that there is no mortality and that every female breeds every year, we will have 70 birds in year two, 430 birds in year three, 2,590 in year four, and 15,550 in year five. By year eight we would have 3,359,230 prairie-chickens. Ecologists call this exponential growth. Zero mortality rarely if ever happens, but this does demonstrate how fast populations can potentially grow.

In 1881, approximately two dozen ring-necked pheasants were introduced to the Willamette Valley in Oregon. A few more birds (nobody is sure of the number) were released in 1882 and 1884. By 1892, on the opening day of the country's first pheasant season, hunters harvested 50,000 birds. It's estimated that as many as a quarter to a half million birds were harvested over the season. If we assume that only a fraction of the population was harvested, that means it grew from a couple dozen to probably several million or more in about a decade. Under the right conditions, wildlife populations can grow tremendously fast.

> [Indiana] Game Commissioner Miles in his 1913 report says that the 1909 legislature closed the season on chickens because there were only a very few left in the state. By 1912, he says, the birds had increased and spread eastward, repopulating 27 new counties in the brief space of four years. His report concludes that at least one third of the 92 counties have chickens, and there are certainly more than 100,000 in the state. (Leopold 1931)

Wildlife populations can crash just as fast. Sadly, twenty years later, only 150 prairie-chickens remained in Indiana (Esten 1933).

For the following scenarios, assume a stable habitat base: the acres of habitat aren't changing. Populations have to deal with predation, competition from similar species, internal and external parasites, and variability in food resources, habitat conditions, and the weather, to name just a few. These factors all interact. The following are some scenarios.

Scenario 1: Bad weather in the summer leads to less available food in the fall and winter. This weakens the birds and their immune systems, which allows an outbreak of parasites. These parasites further weaken the birds, making them more vulnerable to predators and bad weather later in the winter. The population crashes.

Scenario 2: A warm spring and a relatively dry nesting season follow a mild winter. A few summer showers come along at just the right time to produce very good cover. At the same time, a mange outbreak in the local fox population lowers their numbers. Nest success and chick survival are both very high, and the population increases dramatically.

One factor we have little control over and can't manage very easily involves diseases and parasites. This can sometimes interact with food resources. If animals are spread out over the landscape, they won't come into contact with each other much. Therefore, it's hard to transmit diseases or parasites from one individual to another. Oftentimes, especially during harsh winters, people try to feed wildlife. This concentrates individuals of a single species into a small area and brings them into contact with each other. In many cases this can increase the spread of diseases. If it happens at the end of the winter when the animals are already weakened, the diseases can spread that much faster.

There are few better ways to start an argument among wildlife biologists and wildlife managers, not to mention hunters, than to bring up the role of predators in controlling populations of game species, whether it is wolves affecting deer, elk, or moose populations or skunks, raccoons, and foxes affecting duck, pheasant, and grouse populations. Western culture has a long tradition of antipredator attitudes. "We'd look out over their pasture, and without saying the grass was nearly ruined by grazing, I'd point out that with a pair of binoculars we could see every rock the size of a golf ball. That meant a predator could see every bird that tried to nest, and that meant there were no more birds anymore. Their solution was European to the core. 'You got a point there. We need to kill them predators'" (O'Brien 2001).

Many scientists have a different view. Paul Errington, the first faculty member of the Iowa Cooperative Fish and Wildlife Research Unit, was one of the country's top predator researchers in prairie wetland habitats. Even though his name is often linked to predator research, his conclusion about trapping predators to enhance their prey populations was that "as reasoning, it provides us with comfortable and satisfying panaceas, but it has an often overlooked factual disadvantage in that this is not the way things are apt to work out" (Errington 1987).

Unfortunately, emotions can get heated on both sides of the debate. Some, even in the scientific and management community, see predators as snarling killers with blood dripping from their fangs. Others see these same species as cute, cuddly, furry symbols of wilderness. The truth, as always, lies in between. Predators are a politically and scientifically complex issue.

The time of life when a prairie-chicken, duck, or songbird is most susceptible to predation is when it is in the egg. The next riskiest time is when a hen is sitting on a nest of eggs.

Predators do kill prairie-chickens and other birds. The question becomes, do they kill enough to affect the overall size of the population? The other factor we have to consider is whether the primary nest predators—red fox, striped skunks, raccoons—are native to the prairies. While some predators such as badgers do consider the true prairie their home, the three species we focus most of our attention on these days are really woodland edge species. They probably never occurred on the prairies in any great numbers, other than along streams and rivers.

We planted trees across the prairie, making ideal perches for hawks, owls, crows, and ravens. Because we planted trees and built and then abandoned houses and other structures, we created ideal den sites for mammalian predators across our midwestern grasslands. By plowing under most of the grass, we left a small percentage of the landscape for grassland-nesting birds. Then, in or next to these small fragments of habitat, we created ideal habitat for their predators. That's not a good recipe for success.

There are data showing that predator control increases nest success for grassland-nesting birds. Nest success for grassland-nesting birds such as ducks is often below 20 percent and frequently below 10 percent (Klett, Shaffer, and Johnson 1988). Duebbert and Kantrud (1974) found that duckling production increased from 1.9 ducklings per acre in untrapped areas to 8.9 ducklings per acre in areas where predators were trapped. Duebbert and Lokemoen (1980) increased nest success to 94 percent by removing nest predators. Pieron and Rowher (2010) increased duck nest success by 1.4 to 1.9 times when trapping predators over township blocks (six by six miles).

Predator removal does have a price, literally. First, trapping is expensive. It requires equipment, gasoline, and knowledgeable people to do the work. Sargeant, Sovada, and Shaffer (1995) found that it cost $1,661 per wildlife area trapped per year. Wildlife areas are, on average, around a couple hundred acres in size. The researchers stated that "managers contemplating initiating predator removal programs . . . should carefully consider the cost-effectiveness of the programs." To be effective, trapping must be done year after year. Predators will quickly recolonize any area within months after trapping stops. This can become expensive for the agency overseeing the program.

At the same time, habitat management also has a price. Buying the land is often the cheapest part. The land may have to be restored to nesting cover, trees and buildings may need to be removed, and then there is the long-term maintenance. Add to that the taxes that need to be paid each year.

Predator control often involves complicated interactions and unforeseen consequences. Coyotes and red fox don't get along well. Where coyotes are present at reasonable densities, they will chase away or kill red fox. Red fox are much greater predators of waterfowl nests than coyotes are. In a study in North Dakota, Sovada, Sargeant, and Grier (1995) measured nest success in areas dominated by coyotes with few red fox and areas with few coyotes and more abundant red fox. The areas dominated by coyotes had a nest success of 32 percent, while areas dominated by red fox had a nest success of 17 percent. If we remove coyotes, we may increase red fox densities and therefore increase nest predation.

Similar studies have been done in western states with coyotes and sage-grouse (Mezquida, Slater, and Benkham 2006). The researchers hypothesized three negative effects of coyote control on sage-grouse. First, there is little evidence that coyotes prey on sage-grouse at a significant level. Second, removing coyotes may increase populations of fox and raven, species that are known to prey on sage-grouse. Third, removing coyotes may also cause increases in jackrabbit populations. A high density of jackrabbits may attract golden eagles to the area, also a significant predator of grouse. High numbers of jackrabbits could also overbrowse the habitat, leading to lower cover for grouse.

Yeatter (1943) found evidence of prairie-chicken eggs being destroyed by ground squirrels. There are also numerous reports in the waterfowl literature of ground squirrels (thirteen-lined, Richardson's, and Franklin's) destroying duck eggs. Ground squirrels have some of the same predators as the birds they themselves prey on. If a predator (fox and coyote) eradication program is implemented, this might cause the population of ground squirrels to increase dramatically. If ground squirrel populations explode, they might do more damage to the nests than would a ground squirrel population kept under control by a larger predator, even if that larger predator were also preying on eggs. "On the other hand, the great majority of species of hawks and owls, as well as predatory mammals, can well be left undisturbed because of their activity in controlling ground squirrels" (Yeatter 1943). Researchers studying the interactions of predators, rodents, and quail in the southeastern states have reached similar conclusions (Elliott 1974).

The next most practical question to ask is, considering our often very restricted budgets, how do we manage our landscapes and wildlife? First, is predation a factor in prairie-chicken population survival?

The presence of normal predator populations along with relatively high populations of prairie chickens on southeastern Illinois farm lands gives a good indication that widespread predator control would be unnecessary or unprofitable in prairie chicken management. (Yeatter 1943)

Predator controls are rarely recommended for North American prairie grouse, even for increasingly threatened and endangered populations living in altered, isolated, or fragmented habitats. (Schroeder and Baydack 2001)

Second, should money be invested in trapping, or should we be investing limited financial resources in habitat work? This includes both increasing habitat and improving the existing habitat base. Remove the predator habitat and, we hope, remove predators permanently. This includes cutting down trees and removing old structures from wildlife areas. In theory, we do this once. While the initial cost will be higher, the long-term costs may be lower.

Wildlife management isn't done in a vacuum; it's always done within a societal context. Everyone concerned about wildlife can support habitat. Many people concerned about wildlife don't respond well to images of animals in traps or snares. While this shouldn't be the primary reason a manager, agency, or program makes a decision, it is something that needs to be considered.

Predator control makes intuitive sense and allows us to be actively engaged in management. Every time trappers find a dead fox, they think they saved all the birds that fox might have killed. Unfortunately, it isn't that simple.

The last factor, and arguably the most important, is the weather, something we can do little about. Flanders-Wanner, White, and McDaniel (2004) built a population model for sharp-tailed grouse in Nebraska with a number of variables. The variables that best predicted population changes were related to weather. Specifically, average temperatures in May and June and precipitation in the first half of the year were positively correlated with sharp-tail populations. June heat-stress days and June days with rainfalls greater than one inch were negatively correlated with sharp-tail populations. A drought index explained the most variability in the population.

In Texas, Morrow et al. (1996) found that Attwater's prairie-chicken populations were inversely correlated with rainfall in April and May, the nesting season. Likewise, populations in Illinois were inversely correlated with rainfall in May (Westemeier et al. 1998). The more rain during the nesting season, the lower the nesting success. Shelford and Yeatter (1955) described a relationship between prairie-chicken populations and rainfall and solar radiation. All of these are factors we have no control over. Indeed, Flanders-Wanner, White, and McDaniel (2004) titled their paper in the *Wildlife Society Bulletin* "Weather and Prairie Grouse: Dealing with Effects beyond Our Control."

Each year *Pheasants Forever* magazine lists predictions for bird numbers in midwestern and Great Plains states. The following are a few excerpts from the winter 2013 issues.

> Iowa: A cool, wet spring that did the pheasant population no favors. In fact, the rainfall during the spring nesting season was the highest in 141 years of recorded state history.

Kansas: The drought has continued to plague the western half of the state and has limited production.

Minnesota: A long winter followed by a cold, wet spring contributed to a significant decrease in Minnesota's pheasant count.

Missouri: Warmer, drier weather this year appeared in June, which likely increased nesting efforts.

Montana: Substantial flood events occurred in early June, which likely had some adverse effects on nests and broods, but also produced exceptional cover and forage during summer.

Nebraska: The severe drought of 2012 continues to impact pheasant populations statewide, mostly through habitat reduction caused by stunted vegetation growth.

North Dakota: A very wet spring probably affected production on all upland gamebirds.

South Dakota: Persistent drought last year and a cold, wet spring this year are significant factors in this year's reduction in pheasant numbers.

These forecasts focus on two issues. The first is the weather over the past year. This includes rainfall during the nesting and brood-rearing periods, severity of winters, and droughts. All of these can kill birds directly or, as noted in Montana and Nebraska, indirectly by affecting the vegetative cover. The second issue every state cites is habitat loss. That topic gets its own chapter; see chapter 10.

Figure 5 shows records of the population at two individual booming grounds, one in Minnesota and one in Kansas. Both grounds are in extensive tracts of managed grassland. In other words, the habitat base around each ground has not changed over the period of the

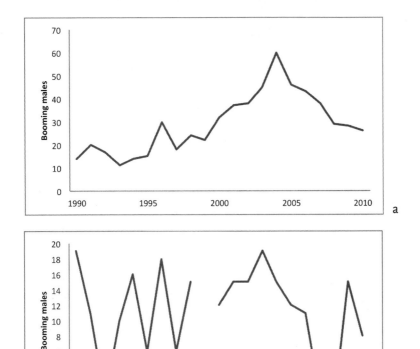

Figure 5. Population at a single booming ground at (a) Bluestem Prairie, Glyndon, Minnesota; and (b) Konza Prairie Biological Station, Manhattan, Kansas. Data courtesy of Brian Winter, The Nature Conservancy, and the Konza Prairie Long-Term Ecological Research program, respectively.

graphs. Even so, the graphs look somewhat chaotic. This can best be explained by the highly variable midwestern weather.

The same principle holds at a number of different scales. Figure 6 shows graphs of populations for areas in North Dakota and Wisconsin, and Figure 7 shows statewide populations for Missouri and Minnesota. At these scales, the fluctuations can represent weather as well

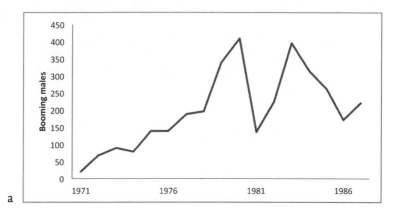

a

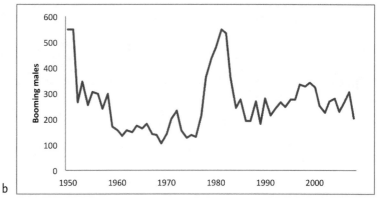

b

Figure 6. Population of (a) Sheyenne National Grassland, southeast North Dakota (Kobriger et al. 1987) and (b) Buena Vista Marsh, Wisconsin (Kardash 2008).

as changes in land use or land cover. The Conservation Reserve Program (CRP) added millions of acres of grass in the 1980s and 1990s. In recent years, many of those acres have been plowed up and planted back to crops. Land use, such as overgrazing caused by a drought on rangelands, can also affect wildlife populations.

The take-home message from each of these graphs is their complexity. It would be difficult to look at any three consecutive years on

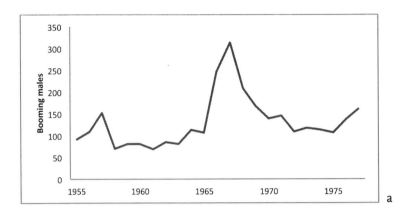

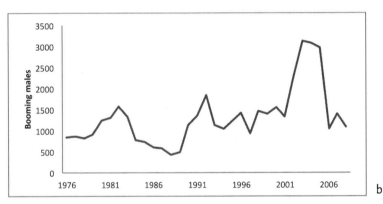

Figure 7. Statewide population in (a) Missouri (Christensen 1981) and (b) Minnesota (courtesy of the Minnesota Prairie Chicken Society and Minnesota Department of Natural Resources).

any of these graphs and predict the fourth year. This is what makes wildlife science and management so challenging.

At any one point in time, a wildlife population is controlled or affected by many different factors singly or in combination: food quality and quantity, predators, disease and parasites, habitat quality and quantity, and the weather. These factors will change seasonally and from year to year. Just as important, many of them are beyond our control. We can't determine ahead of time or affect whether there will be a disease or parasite outbreak in chickens, their prey, or their predators. We don't know what the weather will be like. We don't know how it will affect the birds directly or their habitat and food supply indirectly. Simply changing one factor, by adding food or trapping a few predators, for example, may not affect the overall rate of population change too much.

It can also be difficult to extrapolate study results from one area to another. McNew et al. (2012) titled a paper in the *Journal of Wildlife Management* "Demography of Greater Prairie-Chickens: *Regional Variation* in Vital Rates, Sensitivity Values, and Population Dynamics" (emphasis added).

> Studying both lesser prairie chickens and greater prairie chickens, Jones (1963) asserted that "each species of prairie chicken is adapted to the vegetal character of its region." I suggest this argument could be taken one step further, whereby each population of prairie chicken (in this case greater prairie chicken) is adapted to the character of its region. The results of this study illustrate that GPC do not live in a laboratory, but rather a natural, dynamic environment. (Syrowitz 2013)

Prairie-chickens in Oklahoma face a different environment and limits on their population than birds in northwest Minnesota. Birds in the contiguous grasslands of the Kansas Flint Hills and the fragmented grasslands of Missouri will have different behaviors and factors affecting their population dynamics. Some management ideas we can extrapolate for all prairie-chickens: they need grass. However, the details of population dynamics and habitat management are often regionally specific.

CHAPTER 8

Modern Threats

These birds fly very low in their short flights about the fields, and I am told, hundreds of times they were victims of the wires. Farmers say they have often seen the bodies of the impaled birds hanging on the fences. —*Pierce 1922*

The disappearance of the greater prairie chicken from much of eastern Kansas is attributable to the reduction in native grasslands by plowing and the natural succession of woodlands after prairie fires were excluded. —*Baker 1953*

Smokey the Bear has perhaps been the worst enemy of the prairie chicken. —*Hamerstrom 1980*

Incidentally, when telegraph wires were first installed in the Chicago area, prairie chickens were killed frequently by striking them. —*Schorger 1944*

From a grassland-nesting bird's viewpoint, fires are bad in the short term because they temporarily remove nesting cover and possibly destroy eggs or chicks. In the long term, they are absolutely necessary for maintaining the ecosystem as a grassland instead of a forest or scrubland. One of the primary functions of fire in grasslands is to kill trees. "Had there been no fires, these fine prairies, so marked a feature of the country, would have been covered by the heaviest forest" (Muir 1913). Fortunately, most if not all grassland birds are good renesters if the first nest is lost.

Across the Midwest, fire restrictions keep getting tighter and fire budgets keep getting smaller. All tallgrass prairie plants, birds, and other wildlife are completely dependent on fire. Removing fire from the landscape affects the quality of the remaining grassland. By allowing trees to encroach, lack of fire also decreases the quantity of open grassland habitat.

On the other hand, the idea that the elimination of fire automatically spells an increase of upland game is erroneous: It most often spells their doom. (W. Grange 1939)

The prairie chicken is a doomed species; it will pass from the hunting picture within a few decades at most, and may become extinct in the state [Wisconsin] after 1967. This dismal prediction is inapplicable if management techniques are developed and applied, or if the state experiences widespread accidental fires which again create "barrens" close to wheat and grain. (W. Grange 1948)

While nobody wants "accidental" fires on the landscape, to preserve grasslands and grassland wildlife we need to dramatically increase the use of fire as a management tool across the tallgrass prairie region.

Fire can be a double-edged sword. Sometimes it removes nesting cover or burns up nests. There is a substantial literature showing that grazers are drawn to the lush growth that appears immediately after a fire. Other species of wildlife can also respond almost immediately to fire.

The next day, over this waste would pass little whirlwinds which would lift columns of ashes in inverted cones to a height far out of sight, at the base of which the ground squirrels, prairie chickens, the plovers, and the other denizens of the prairie were eagerly running about to find whatever there was of interest in the swept and garnished landscape. (Quick 1925)

As a result of the stimulation of plant growth after a fire, the area should produce excellent nesting cover in the years following the fire.

In addition to not using fire enough to control tree encroachment, many government programs still promote the planting of trees on the prairie. This started as early as 1873 with the Timber Culture Act, when prairie settlers had to plant trees as part of their homesteading practices.

> This process [forestation] is accentuated and speeded by the widespread practice of planting conifers in the large openings (generally fire created) and to some extent upon abandoned farm lands. When natural forest reproduction or artificial planting is responsible for the reversion, the result in terms of prairie chickens and sharp-tails is the same: *Disappearance or exclusion*. (W. Grange 1948; emphasis in the original)

It's often very difficult to sell people on the idea that trees are detrimental. Planting trees is good. We all did it as Girl Scouts or Boy Scouts. Planting trees is often sold as reforesting. The problem is that you can't reforest an area that was never forested to begin with. Today, many government agencies still plant trees in prairies for wildlife habitat or winter cover. And yes, those trees will provide habitat for wildlife—the issue is which species of wildlife.

Those rows of trees will provide habitat for generalist species of wildlife that are already abundant, such as blue jays and chickadees, while removing habitat from specialist species of wildlife that need very specific types of habitat, such as grassland birds. Once the trees are planted and established, their seeds rain into the neighboring prairie. Soon a narrow line of trees becomes a small forest.

This is not a new problem. As far back as the early 1800s, settlers were commenting on how quickly trees were invading the prairies. Settlers were already changing the landscape at this early date (Pyne 1982).

Trees provide a number of problems for ground-nesting birds. For one thing, trees are a visual obstruction on the horizon. Several species of grassland birds simply avoid nesting near trees. In addition, trees provide ideal homes for predators.

Researchers in northeastern Colorado studied nest success in pheasants. They found that within 640 yards of trees only 14 percent of the nests were successful. Nests farther away from trees had a success rate of 33 percent (W. Snyder 1984). Trees cut nest success in half. A circle with a radius of 640 yards covers 270 acres. That means that for every tree, windbreak, or woodlot in grassland bird nesting areas, 270 acres become high-risk areas for nest success.

Mammalian predators living in hollow trunks can wander about the nearby prairie and consume any eggs they find. One investigation in Missouri found that only three of seventeen prairie-chicken nests (18 percent) survived when woody cover around the nest was only 5 percent. When woody cover was below 5 percent, fifteen of twenty-six nests (58 percent) successfully hatched eggs (McKee, Ryan, and Mechlin 1998). Prairie-chickens are three times more successful at nesting without trees. Practically every study ever done on grassland-nesting birds—songbirds, pheasants, grouse, and waterfowl—has shown detrimental effects of trees.

While predation may or may not affect overall population levels, grassland birds live in such a small part of the midwestern landscape that we need to make sure that all of those acres are as productive as possible. The debate then gets back to eliminating predator habitat or removing predators directly.

Another cause of mortality in prairie-chickens is collision with fences and utility lines. Toepfer (2003) estimated that as much as 4 to 14 percent of prairie-chicken mortality was caused by collision with wires. Working with lesser prairie-chickens, D. Wolfe (2006) determined that 42.8 percent and 26.5 percent of mortality in Oklahoma and New Mexico, respectively, resulted from collisions with fences or utility lines. And those numbers are probably low.

Unless the birds are wearing radio transmitters as part of a research project, several things have to happen for people to find a carcass. First, they have to see the well-camouflaged body hidden in the grass. Second, they have to walk by soon after the bird hits the wire, before the carcass is found by a scavenger. Furthermore, they will find only the birds that hit the wires and died instantly. What about those birds that hit the wire, wander off dazed and crippled, and are easy prey for the next predator that walks or wings by? They will never be found. The numbers of birds that fall victim to wires can be significant.

> Even as late as 1874, many birds were killed every winter by flying against the telegraph wires along the railroad. (Hornaday 1904)

> Toward the end of the century the erection of the phone and telegraph lines and wire fences took a heavy toll on the low-flying prairie fowl flocks. (Stempel and Rodgers 1961)

Many of these birds eventually made it to the dinner table.

> The Iowa Game Survey (1932) quotes old timers who after each stormy evening made it a practice to pick up gunny sacks full of prairie chickens under the telegraph lines. (Leopold 1933)

> The great numbers of prairie chickens killed by hitting the new wires provided a ready supply of meat for the construction workers. (Ligon 1951)

The numbers again point to the large populations of prairie-chickens. Only a small percentage of a flock is going to hit the wires. When even this small percentage is enough to fill gunny sacks or feed entire construction crews, we have to wonder how large the entire flock was.

Fence line collisions point to the need to carefully consider grazing management in the context of grassland birds. Any grazing will need a perimeter fence. The number and type of internal cross-fences can be constructed with wildlife in mind. Fortunately, researchers in Oklahoma are developing ways to mark fences to make them more visible to low-flying prairie-chickens (D. Wolfe, Patten, and Sherrod 2009).

Another emerging threat to all grassland birds, as well as bats, is wind energy development. Every bird lover is interested in moving the economy toward green or renewable energy. And wind should be a major player in our energy strategy, especially in the windy Great Plains and Midwest. The problem for birds is reflected by the old real estate adage "location, location, location."

Many counties in the Midwest classify rural land for taxes as either agricultural or waste, which includes grasslands, brush, pastures, and so forth. Row-crop fields are seen as productive, but grass is just grass. To a developer, one of the best ways to exploit wastelands is to make them produce energy. Also, a lot of the remaining unplowed prairies are on hilltops and ridges—places that are too high, too dry, too rocky, or too steep to plow. Those same hilltops also happen to be some of the windiest places. Therefore, many of the last remaining tracts of prairie are being targeted for wind farms (Kuvelsky et al. 2007).

Wind turbines create three problems for grassland birds. The first, and probably smallest, problem is direct collision with the turbine blades. Those blades look like they are turning slowly. However, the tips of some of them are moving as fast as 120 miles per hour. In numerous studies, bird carcasses have been collected at the base of wind towers, and the death toll can be startling, especially during peak songbird migration (Leddy, Higgins, and Naugle 1999; Osborn et al. 2000; G. Johnson et al. 2002; Kunz et al. 2007). Second, turbines create the same vertical structure as trees, and some grassland bird species may avoid potential nesting habitat near turbines just as they avoid grass near trees. The last, and possibly largest, impact on grassland birds is the infrastructure associated with wind farms. Wind farms are more than just towers: there are transmission lines, utility buildings, access roads, traffic, noise, and so forth. Prairie grouse generally avoid all of these (Robel et al. 2004; Pitman et al. 2005). Roads remove and fragment grassland habitat, disturb wildlife, and provide easy access points for predators. Winder et al. (2014) found that the home range size of prairie-chicken hens doubled near turbines and that females generally avoided areas with turbines. The increased home range of hens with broods can lead to lower survival, as the birds have to travel farther to find food. Increased home range size and movement may cost the chicks energy that could be used for growth and may expose them to higher predation risks.

Researchers in Oklahoma found that prairie-chickens avoid power lines. They found no prairie-chickens within one hundred meters of lines and only five locations within five hundred meters (Pruett, Patten, and Wolfe 2009). What this does is create a buffer or no-man's-land along power line corridors. There is grassland habitat underneath and near these lines, but the birds won't use these areas. Across the Midwest there are millions of acres of corn and soybean fields, which provide little to no habitat for wildlife. Placing turbines in these already heavily developed and modified landscapes would be good for everyone—farmers, consumers, and birds. Some environmental groups have lobbied against turbines because of their damage to bird populations, but the answer isn't to halt development. The answer is to work with developers to move the turbines into areas where they will still produce clean energy but will be less damaging to wildlife and habitat.

Pesticides are yet another threat to prairie-chickens and other grassland birds. Birds in fragmented habitat will be more exposed than those living in large contiguous grasslands such as the Sand Hills of Nebraska or the Flint Hills of Kansas. Pesticides can drift from adjacent fields onto conservation lands, and the smaller these areas are, the smaller the area away from the edge, where pesticide drift is most problematic.

Pesticides can have direct and indirect effects on grassland birds. First, insects are the primary prey for young birds. If all the insects are killed by insecticides, there will be less food available for fast-growing chicks. Second, birds can pick up chemicals that have drifted onto the vegetation from neighboring row-crop fields, or they can eat insects that have sublethal doses of the chemicals. Many insecticides are neurotoxins and have been shown to have neurological effects on vertebrate animals, especially in developing embryos.

Across the range of the prairie-chicken, we have removed most of their grassland habitat. The remaining grassland is in small fragments scattered across the landscape. We often build hostile habitat (trees, abandoned buildings, turbines, power lines) adjacent to these grasslands. Finally, we spray toxic chemicals on the adjacent crop-lands that often drift into the desirable habitat.

Rachel Carson's *Silent Spring* was one of the first books to raise concern about chemicals in the environment. Unfortunately, in the decades since then, focus on this topic somewhat waned. However, around 2008 a focus emerged on a new class of insecticides called neonicotinoids. Published research on the environmental effects of these chemicals increased dramatically in 2013 and 2014.

Neonicotinoids are based on the nicotine compound found in tobacco. Nicotine is a neurotoxin. It works by overexciting the nervous system, leading to paralysis, which leads to death (Fishel 2013). Neonicotinoid use in the United States has grown from essentially zero in 1994 to just under half a million pounds in 2003. In 2004 farmers used just under one and a half million pounds. That number grew to just under three and a half million pounds in 2009 (Hopwood et al. 2013). Between 2009 and 2013, neonicotinoid use more than doubled again across much of the Midwest (Hladik, Kolpin, and Kuivila 2014).

Neonicotinoids are used in several ways. One of the most common methods is pretreatment of the seed before planting. As the seed germinates, it absorbs the chemical, which then spreads throughout all parts of the plant. This is meant to deter herbivorous insects that eat the crop. However, a lot of the chemical leaches into the soil or becomes airborne when the seed is jostled around in the seeding equipment.

During seeding, some seed is spilled on the ground or does not get planted as deep as it should. Goulson (2013) reviewed a series of studies that showed that after planting there is sufficient neonicotinoid-treated seed on the ground to produce a lethal dose to 50 percent of a population of forty partridges per acre. A partridge is a European game bird slightly smaller than a prairie-chicken. A lethal dose to 50 percent of a population, the LD_{50}, is a common way to describe the toxicity of a drug or chemical. Presumably the 50 percent that survive will be quite sick. Multiply that by the acres of corn and soybeans planted across the Midwest.

These chemicals are becoming common and persistent in the environment. Hladik, Kolpin, and Kuivila (2014) published a paper titled

"Widespread Occurrence of Neonicotinoid Insecticides in Streams in a High Corn and Soybean Producing Region, USA." Earlier that same year, Main et al. (2014) published a paper titled "Widespread Use and Frequent Detection of Neonicotinoid Pesticides in Wetlands of Canada's Prairie Pothole Region." Studies in England have found that the chemicals persist in the soil long after the seed is planted; in some cases, the chemical was still detected in the soil three years after it was last used in a field (A. Jones, Harrington, and Turnbull 2014).

Neonicotinoids and other pesticides can affect wildlife in several ways (Boatman et al. 2004; Gibbons, Morrissey, and Mineau 2014). First, there can be direct mortality from being sprayed with the chemicals. This can happen if young chicks are foraging along the edge of a field or in an adjacent ditch when the field is sprayed. Second, the insecticides can remove insects, a key component of the birds' diets, from the landscape. Birds then have to work harder and travel farther to find enough insects to survive. Last, and perhaps worst, is cumulative sublethal exposure to these chemicals.

The birds may rub against vegetation that has some chemical on it or drink some water or dew that has the chemical in it. They will slowly accumulate the chemical in their bodies as they do this day after day. Additionally, they may eat insects that themselves were exposed to sublethal doses of the chemical. Birds eat thousands of insects in their first few weeks. Even small amounts of chemical in each insect, multiplied by thousands or tens of thousands of insects, will produce a relatively high concentration of chemicals in the birds' bodies.

Once in the birds' bodies, the chemicals can affect their nervous systems. It's hard to fly, forage, or escape predators if you lack muscle coordination. Researchers have found that one of the most dangerous times for an animal to be exposed to these chemicals is as a fetus. The time when the brain and nervous system are growing and developing is a bad time to expose an animal to a neurotoxin.

Going one step past wildlife, the European Food Safety Authority (2013) concluded that neonicotinoids "may affect neuronal development and function" in humans. Kimura-Kuroda et al. (2012) determined that "therefore, the neonicotinoids may be adversely affecting human health, especially the developing brain." One can only imagine the fetal developmental issues of small species of wildlife living in the habitats that are sprayed and eating seeds treated with these chemicals. Results from Tokumoto et al. (2013), studying quail in Japan, indicated "the possibility that neonicotinoid severely affects the reproductive function in quails."

Mineau and Whiteside (2013) published a paper titled "Pesticide Acute Toxicity Is a Better Correlate of U.S. Grassland Bird Declines Than Agricultural Intensification." Similarly, Mason et al. (2012) published a paper titled "Immune Suppression by Neonicotinoid Insecticides at the Root of Global Wildlife Declines." Sadly, one doesn't even need to read the papers to understand the general results.

CHAPTER 9

Managing Populations

Even though some of these statements may be exag-
geration, there is no doubt these birds were once
almost unbelievably abundant. —*Schwartz 1945*

It is not unthinkable, or even improbable, that a future generation
of Wisconsin citizens may dedicate a bronze plaque and monument to the memory of our vanished chickens and sharp-tails
even as we dedicated a monument to the wild pigeon in Wyalus-
ing State Park in 1947 with the thought in mind that "it shall not
happen again" for other native species. —*W. Grange 1948*

Thus, Iowa, which once had some of the finest prairie habitat in
North America and was at the very center of the greater prairie-chicken's Midwest range, no longer supports a native population
of the bird most symbolic of prairie habitat. —*Dinsmore 1994*

For the ghosts of prairie grouse that were the last vestiges of a population, there is a special sadness. It didn't need to happen. —*Berg 2004*

While the reduction of the uncountable flocks of passenger pigeons
and vast herds of bison were the wildlife tragedies of the nineteenth
century, the prairie-chicken is one of the great tragedies of twentieth-
century wildlife management and agricultural practices in this
country. The heath hen is extinct, the Attwater's is barely hanging
on, and the greater prairie-chicken is greatly reduced in numbers and
geographic range.

I saw in October more birds rise out of a forty acre field than the cities of the Union could consume in a month. (Merritt 1904)

Flocks of prairie chickens, vast enough to darken the skies as they flew. (quoted in Faragher 1986)

How can a species go from unimaginable numbers to extinction across 90 percent of its former range? Westemeier (1985) estimated that there may have been as many as fourteen million prairie-chickens in Illinois alone in the mid-1800s. In 2011, the continental population of mallards, the most common duck, was estimated at nine million.

Large populations are relatively easy to manage, whereas small populations create a number of challenges for managers. The smaller the population, the higher the probability that purely random events, over which managers and society have no control, will drop the population's number to zero, and it will become locally extinct. The larger the population, the lower the probability that it will disappear, because if the numbers drop, plenty of individuals still remain.

In Illinois, one isolated population of prairie-chickens increased from 40 to 206 males between the mid-1960s and the early 1970s on only 660 acres of habitat. By 1994, researchers could only find 6 males (Westemeier, Simpson, and Esker 1999). This population was isolated from any other population, so no birds could move in from surrounding areas to help replenish the population.

Isolated relict populations, such as greater prairie chickens in Illinois, cannot be conserved indefinitely with inadequate habitat and small size. (Westemeier et al. 1998)

When there is a continuous distribution of individuals over a large area, local-scale mortality events aren't a problem in the long run. Imagine that a late March blizzard hits an area the size of several counties. The birds have struggled through an entire winter and have used up all their fat stores. All, or almost all, of the birds in the area die. For the next two years, bird density in this area will be very low. However, birds can move into the affected area from all directions. In another two or three years, population density will be back to where it was before the blizzard. The neighboring state has a small, isolated population. A similar storm hits the area, and all the birds die. Now, there are no birds in the surrounding areas to recolonize the affected area and the species becomes locally extinct.

Imagine a large population, a million birds. The storm mentioned kills 90 percent of the birds. That still leaves one hundred thousand birds. A series of good breeding years and the population is back to where it started. If it's a large regional population, additional birds can fly in from the edges to help the population increase. Now imagine a small, isolated population of one hundred birds. An ice storm hits and only 10 percent, ten birds, survive. By dumb luck, maybe the survivors are all male or all female. Or only a couple of the remaining ten are female. In the first case, the effective population size is zero since none can breed. In the second case, the effective population size is very small. Because the population is isolated, no birds can fly in from neighboring areas.

As populations become smaller, they lose both individuals and genes. In the long run, the loss of genes may be more important than the loss of an individual. Small populations have lower levels of genetic diversity than large populations simply because of the random loss of genes. Scientists refer to this as genetic drift.

In the most extreme case, imagine that every member of a small population dies, except one brood of prairie-chickens. Once these chicks reach maturity, they can breed only with a sibling or a parent. Even if the population increases in size, the larger population will still have a low level of genetic diversity. Every bird in the population will be a close relative. Scientists refer to this as a bottleneck, and prairie-chicken populations in some states have bottlenecked several times.

Overall, these results strongly support the idea that the Illinois population originally had higher levels of genetic diversity that were consequently lost through its demographic contraction during the last century. (Bouzat, Lewin, and Paige 1998)

Low genetic diversity can lead to increased susceptibility to disease and parasites. Everyone is familiar with flu season. We also know that among any group of people, some seem to never get sick, some have a runny nose for a couple of days, and some people are flat on their back for several days. Each person is genetically unique, and each person's genes give him or her different levels of resistance to any particular flu virus. The person who didn't get sick at all from this year's flu strain may be in bed for a week with next year's flu strain. In a wildlife population with low genetic diversity, all the individuals will be vulnerable to the same strains of infection or parasites. If the right virus, bacteria, or parasite hits that population, the pathogen could wipe it out.

Population contraction can also be related to habitat contraction. In the Illinois example, all the birds were living in a few blocks of habitat. A lit cigarette out the car window during the nesting season could doom that population. This is exactly what happened to the last population of the heath hen, isolated on Martha's Vineyard. One fire played a part in driving the entire species to extinction. In 1916 estimates of the heath hen population on the island ranged from 800 to 2,000 birds. That year a wildfire swept the island. In 1917, only 150 were found. While the population rebounded to 600 within three years, by 1927 only 13 birds were counted. The next year the population was down to 3 (Hough 1933), and the species was extinct four years later.

As a species' range contracts, the effect isn't simply like a bubble deflating: the population fragments. Even when the prairie-chicken's range was at its maximum, the population was not evenly distributed. The birds were found at higher density in some areas, at lower density in others, and in still others not at all. As the species' range contracted, the population in the low-density areas became locally extinct and that in the high-density areas became isolated.

Figure 8 shows a map of the prairie-chicken's range in 1969. In the years since this map was published, the populations in Michigan,

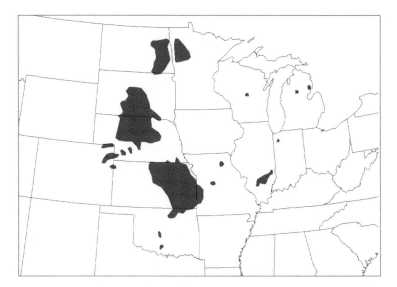

Figure 8. Range of prairie-chickens in the late 1960s. Adapted from Christisen (1969).

Indiana, and southern Oklahoma have all probably gone extinct. The populations in Illinois and Wisconsin are still hanging on. However, managers have transported hundreds of birds into these states from neighboring states. Without this artificial boost, the populations in these states would probably be locally extinct.

The Missouri and Wisconsin prairie-chicken populations have been highly fragmented for much of the last century. The maps in figures 9 and 10 show the effects of fragmentation on regional populations. Most or all of the small populations in the earlier maps are gone in the later maps. Most of the large populations have shrunk in size or fragmented into multiple small populations. This is a general pattern for all wildlife once their habitat becomes broken into small fragments scattered around a larger landscape. Unfortunately, most of these areas are too far from their nearest neighbor for birds to fly from one area to another. This means each area is genetically isolated and inbreeding will increase. Also, if the population crashes, there is a low probability that the area can be recolonized from neighboring

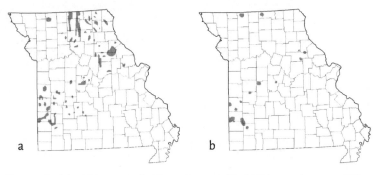

Figure 9. Prairie-chicken range in Missouri, mapped by (a) Schwartz in 1945 and (b) Johnsgard in 2002.

populations. Comparing the maps, we can easily imagine what will happen to all the small populations on the most recent maps without a serious conservation effort.

This leads us to the concept of the metapopulation, which is a population of populations. A large block of grass habitat holds several booming grounds. All the birds in this area constitute a population. We can measure population size and changes in population, birth rates, and mortality each year. The next population of prairie-chickens may be several miles away. And another population is a few miles beyond that one. We can measure the populations of each of these areas separately and independently.

Sometimes a bird will fly from one area to another, emigrating from one area and immigrating into another. The bird has increased the population size in the new area and has potentially increased the genetic diversity there by bringing in new genes. While each area is generally self-contained, a few birds move from one area or population to another each year.

Earlier, we saw how a storm could wipe out a local population. With a metapopulation, this becomes less problematic. Within the next year or so, some birds will fly into the vacant area from neighboring areas. After a few years, these immigrant birds will establish a new breeding population in that area.

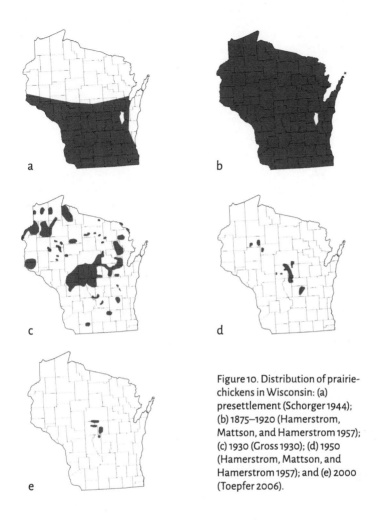

Figure 10. Distribution of prairie-chickens in Wisconsin: (a) presettlement (Schorger 1944); (b) 1875–1920 (Hamerstrom, Mattson, and Hamerstrom 1957); (c) 1930 (Gross 1930); (d) 1950 (Hamerstrom, Mattson, and Hamerstrom 1957); and (e) 2000 (Toepfer 2006).

In Wisconsin, prairie-chickens are concentrated into four management units. In the 1950s, there was enough open country between the units that birds frequently moved back and forth, creating one large population. The closest booming grounds between the northern and southern areas were about five miles apart in the 1960s. Today, because of residential development and tree encroachment, the closest booming grounds are about fourteen miles apart, and there appears to be little movement between the northern and southern areas (J. Johnson et al. 2004). The Wisconsin population was relatively small to begin with and isolated by several hundred miles from the next closest population in western Minnesota. Now it appears that there are actually two small populations acting in isolation instead of one larger metapopulation with birds moving between the four areas.

Metapopulations can have several advantages in wildlife conservation, especially in the agriculturally dominated Midwest. In the Intermountain West, some species such as grizzly bears need vast tracts of continuous habitat to survive. In the Midwest, we will probably never restore thousands of contiguous square miles of grass, but we can create patches of two hundred acres here and three hundred acres there across the landscape.

This is where bird conservation has a distinct advantage over mammal, reptile, or amphibian conservation. When we want to connect isolated populations of wildlife that can't fly, we have to build a continuous strip of habitat connecting one area to another. These strips are called corridors. What happens if a city or an interstate or a landowner who isn't interested in conservation is in that corridor?

Prairie-chickens and other birds can fly or hopscotch from one area to another. We can define a corridor on a map, but instead of restoring all the land in that corridor, we need only make sure there is at least some habitat every few miles. If some landowners don't want to sell to a wildlife agency or enroll their land in a conservation program, maybe their neighbors will. Birds can fly right over highways and interstates.

Eventually, we can connect all these habitats and populations throughout a region. While no one bird would travel the entire length of the region, their genes can. One individual can travel to a new area, its offspring can travel to the next area, and so on. In this way, a series of local populations can function as one large regional population. Genes can be exchanged over long distances, minimizing inbreeding or genetic drift.

This helps wildlife managers plan where they can get the biggest return from their work. For instance, wildlife managers have enough resources to purchase and restore six hundred acres of prairie. Where do they want to purchase those acres? They can buy land next to an existing area of grassland to make it larger. They can also buy land between two areas of grassland habitat to make it easier for birds to move from one established area to another.

When we discuss populations, in addition to the overall count of individuals, or the total population, there is also the effective population, often abbreviated as "Ne." This is the number of breeding individuals. This becomes especially important when studying lek-breeding species like prairie-chickens, in which only a few males do the majority of the breeding (Ballard and Robel 1974). The effective population can be substantially smaller than the censused population. J. Johnson et al. (2004) determined that the effective breeding population was only 5 to 16 percent of the census estimates in Wisconsin prairie-chickens.

In the scientific and conservation literature, determining the minimum viable genetic population for wildlife is its own subdiscipline, with many published papers for many species. The best estimate is that it takes five hundred to five thousand individuals in a breeding population to maintain genetic diversity (Franklin 1980; Lande and Barrowclough 1987; Lande 1995; Franklin and Frankham 1998; Lynch and Lande 1998). J. Johnson, Toepfer, and Dunn (2003) suggest that prairie-chicken populations below two thousand will lose genetic variation.

We can start to make some guesstimates of what it would take to conserve a genetically diverse population of prairie-chickens. A number of assumptions need to be made, and every number or assumption in the following calculation can be picked apart. But this is a place to start. Assume an even gender ratio with equal numbers of males and females (Schroeder and Robb 1993). The average size of booming grounds is roughly ten males. Because of the lek breeding system, the top two males on a booming ground do roughly 90 percent of the breeding (Ballard and Robel 1974). Therefore, only 20 percent of the males are part of the effective or breeding population. (J. Johnson et al. [2004] found this number to be even smaller.) That means the effective population size is twelve individuals, two males and ten females. We therefore need approximately 170 booming grounds to have a population of two thousand individuals. Each booming ground needs at least 320 acres of grass, so we need 54,400 acres of grass on the landscape, preferably evenly distributed in relatively large blocks.

This manages for the minimum, which is a recipe for disaster. The Attwater's prairie-chicken working group is managing for the possibility of two catastrophic years in a row. A catastrophic year is defined as zero recruitment into the population from the year's hatch, or 100 percent nest failure. Since roughly 50 percent of the adult birds die each year, a catastrophic year would cut the population in half. Therefore, we can multiply our acreage by four to account for two bad years in a row. This gives us 216,600 acres to support an effective breeding population of eight thousand birds. Ideally, this would be in 320-acre blocks every square mile, for a total of 680 square miles, or nineteen townships. Additionally, all that grass has to be managed favorably for prairie-chickens. This is a very simple calculation of population and habitat. There are other, far more complex calculations to arrive at more precise estimates of populations and habitat requirements.

What does genetic diversity really mean? Why is more diversity better than less diversity? In the case of prairie-chickens, researchers have actually measured this. In Illinois, Westemeier et al. (1998) measured population size, egg fertility, and hatch rate of prairie-chickens from the early 1960s to the early 1990s. As the population size decreased, genetic diversity decreased. As genetic diversity decreased, the fertility and hatch rate of eggs decreased. Peterson and Silvy (1996) found that hatch rates in Attwater's prairie-chickens declined from greater than 90 percent in the 1930s to 50 percent in the 1980s. As a population gets smaller, it becomes harder for it to grow larger because of the low hatch rate. However, Bellinger et al. (2003) did not find declines in hatch rates in Wisconsin with smaller populations. This may be because these populations were just large enough to avoid hitting some critical threshold.

This can set up what scientists call an extinction vortex. Start with a small population that is suffering from inbreeding and genetic drift, both of which lead to a loss of genetic diversity. That low genetic diversity can lead to lower reproductive rates and sicker animals less able to fight off pathogens. This will make the future population even smaller. The cycle continues, with the population continuing to decrease until it becomes locally extinct.

There are a number of wildlife success stories in the conservation literature. Peregrine falcons were virtually wiped out from the continental United States in the days of DDT. After decades of hard work, falcons can be seen across most of their former range. Probably the best-known reintroduction is the wolf to Yellowstone National Park. This population has grown to the point that there are now packs across several western states. Unfortunately, reintroduction efforts with prairie-chickens have had varying or limited success (J. Snyder, Pelren, and Crawford 1999).

In Illinois, 518 prairie-chickens were trapped in nearby states and released between 1992 and 1998 to supplement the small existing population (Westemeier, Simpson, and Esker 1999). By 1998, the number of displaying males in booming ground counts had increased to 84 in one area from a low of 6 birds. However, this is still far below the minimum number needed.

Iowa has a similar story (Moe 1999). In 1980 and 1982, a total of 101 prairie-chickens were released. No birds were found after 1984. Between 1990 and 1994, a total of 549 prairie-chickens were released. In 1995, only 40 males were observed, and the number dropped to 26 in 1996.

Over the past decade, Minnesota has moved hundreds of birds from the northwestern part of the state to the west-central part. Each year, after the releases are completed, the number of males counted on booming grounds decreases by 50 percent. Today, the introduced population is presumed extinct.

There are two types of introductions. In the first case, birds are introduced to an area where there are not currently any birds. The second type of introduction is often called a genetic rescue. For example, a small population of birds in an area is suffering genetically as a result of genetic drift and inbreeding. New birds are brought in or, more appropriately, new genes are brought in to increase the genetic diversity of the local population.

There are a few caveats to introductions or reintroductions. For one, the habitat base should be capable of supporting a genetically viable population in the new area. Also, genetically viable populations need a large number of individuals. If only a small population of birds is translocated to an isolated area, in the long term the population will still suffer from isolation, genetic drift, and inbreeding. The hope is that once the population becomes established, it will increase in size. However, the larger population may still suffer from the small gene pool of the original population.

Most grouse reintroduction projects move primarily females to the new population. Because of the lek breeding structure of prairie-chickens, any new males brought into the area would probably find themselves on the edge of the lek and would not breed. New genes will come into the population only if the new birds breed with the existing population.

The next issue is to evaluate why that population declined there originally. Are there enough acres of habitat? Is it too isolated from other populations? Pheasant nest parasitism can be very high (Westemeier et al. 1998). If prairie-chickens are brought into the area during a peak in the pheasant population, the rate of nest parasitism may be so high that the birds will have such low reproductive rates that the population won't survive.

Although translocations may be an effective management strategy for the overall genetic restoration of endangered wild populations, their long-term viability cannot be guaranteed unless we take into consideration the demographic and environmental factors that have led to the original species decline. (Bouzat et al. 2009)

Several studies have focused on the restoration of the genetic diversity of an existing population of prairie-chickens, most notably in Illinois and Wisconsin. The first issue with translocations is how similar the birds from the source population are to those in the population to be helped. It's good to increase diversity, but we don't want to introduce genes that might negatively affect the population. For instance, Wisconsin introduced birds from western Minnesota.

Both populations are in cold, relatively wet northern areas. Presumably the birds from Minnesota had genes that would be good in Wisconsin. However, prairie-chickens (and their genes) in Oklahoma are going to be adapted to a hotter, drier prairie. Introducing Oklahoma birds into Wisconsin could potentially bring in genes that could in the long-term hurt the Wisconsin population (Edmands 2007).

Researchers are still experimenting with methods of reintroduction, such as the time of year the birds are released and the number of birds released. Translocations and reintroductions are still valuable conservation tools, but as with anything in wildlife management, they are more complicated than they originally sound.

Populations of all wildlife fluctuate unpredictably from year to year from a number of influences. Prairie-chickens eat hundreds of species of insects, leaves, seeds, and fruit. The abundance of any one of these will fluctuate from season to season and year to year as a result of rainfall, temperature, agricultural policy and commodity markets, and other factors. Prairie-chickens compete directly or indirectly with sharp-tailed grouse, pheasants, and other grassland birds for food and space. At different stages of their lives, prairie-chickens are preyed upon by hawks, owls, eagles, crows, magpies, skunks, raccoons, foxes, coyotes, ground squirrels, and other species.

Disease and parasites can affect the foods prairie-chickens eat, as well as the prairie-chickens themselves, the species prairie-chickens compete with, and the predators that eat prairie-chickens. Weather, such as severe winters, rainstorms during nesting season, or droughts during brood-rearing season, affects all wildlife. A crash in food resources may cause a population to starve. A crash in the predator population may help a population increase.

There are dozens to hundreds of factors that directly or indirectly affect prairie-chickens. Write "prairie-chicken" in the center of a piece of paper. On the bottom half of the paper, write every plant and insect they might eat. To the right and left of "prairie-chicken," write all the species they might compete with. Next, at the top of the page, list every predator of prairie-chickens. Now, start drawing connections. Prairie-chickens eat plants and the insects that also eat plants. Foxes and coyotes eat prairie-chickens, but coyotes also eat foxes. Next, list all the diseases and parasites for each species on your piece of paper. Last, list all the different types of weather that can affect wildlife. Again, start drawing lines. What you end up with very quickly is a complex spiderweb of lines going everywhere.

We have the ability to control only a few of these factors or the interactions between them. With all these factors interacting, the population will fluctuate from year to year. Large populations can fluctuate up and down and still be safe. If a small population fluctuates too much, there is a good possibility that a decline will go all the way to zero and the species will become locally extinct. We can't control most of these factors, but one factor we can control is habitat.

CHAPTER 10

Managing Habitat

No game bird has shown greater adaptability to environment
than the prairie chicken. From time to time they have changed
their habits to conform to the advance of civilization. And today, if
given sufficient protection to enable them to rear their young and
to attain strength of wing and feather, they will take care of themselves in any country that they formerly inhabited. —*Bruette 1916*

The future of the prairie chicken in Missouri is in the
hands of all people of the state, but it depends most of
all upon those who use the soil. —*Schwartz 1945*

Prairie chickens are essentially birds of grasslands. Fortunately,
the practices recommended for the most profitable long-time use
of grasslands are beneficial to prairie chickens. —*Baker 1953*

The fact that the prairie chickens have done so well here
[Buena Vista Marsh, Wisconsin] for so many years is good
evidence that prairie chickens and people can live quite closely
together. —*Hamerstrom, Mattson, and Hamerstrom 1957*

Prairie-chickens are birds of large landscapes (Niemuth 2003) and
complex habitats. Land use, such as agricultural practices, has been
written about extensively. Research papers with the phrases "land
use" or "habitat use" have been published from Illinois (Yeatter 1963),
Kansas (Arthaud 1970; Robel et al. 1970), North Dakota (Kirsch,
Klett, and Miller 1973), Missouri (Drobney and Sparrowe 1977),
Minnesota (Merrill et al. 1999), and Wisconsin (Niemuth 2000).

However, coordinating management of land use across thousands of public and private acres is very difficult.

We always want to find the easiest answers to any problem. One supposedly easy way to manage populations is through predator control. Predators kill prairie-chickens. Therefore, we should kill predators. Fewer predators equal more prairie-chickens. However, it doesn't often work out like that for prairie-chickens, or for most wildlife species.

> Frederick pointed out that there had been foxes and prairie chickens since time immemorial and what we needed was good brood-nest cover. "Look," he said, finally raising his voice. "It doesn't matter how many foxes there are if the chickens have good habitat! What the prairie chickens need is *land*, not fox trappers." (Hamerstrom 1980)

> Predator removals can benefit fecundity and adult survival of ground-nesting game birds but are expensive, time-consuming, and a short-term solution for a relatively small area. Management actions aimed at reducing the negative impacts of edge effects by increasing the number, size, and proximity of tallgrass prairie fragments will likely be more effective at increasing vital rates, and improving long-term population viability. (McNew et al. 2012)

Put more succinctly:

> It is by now virtually axiomatic that strong environment is the most practicable defense against predators. (Hamerstrom, Mattson, and Hamerstrom 1957)

This principle applies to more than just chickens. Aldo Leopold and Herb Stoddard are two of the fathers of game management. Leopold (1933) stated, "Better food and cover represents, in many instances, the cheapest and most effective predator insurance." At the same time, working with quail in the southeast, Stoddard (1931) stated, "Where cover and food supply are adequate, great reproductive powers usually enable the bobwhites to maintain themselves against their natural enemies."

Wildlife need habitat, lots of it. They need a large quantity of high-quality habitat. One of the primary goals of conservation is to provide a large enough habitat base so that when a population undergoes random and unpredictable drops because of the weather, predators, parasites, diseases, or any other factor, it still has a significant number of individuals.

How much is enough when it comes to prairie-chickens and grass? That question has several different answers.

Big blocks of habitat provide several advantages for both prairie-chickens and the grassland-breeding bird community in general. As the size of the grassland increases, the number of bird species found in the grassland also increases (Herkert 1994; Helzer and Zelinski 1999; Winter and Faaborg 1999; Walk and Warner 1999). There are probably several reasons for this pattern. First, some species won't nest in small blocks of habitat because there just aren't enough resources. The habitat block must be large enough to accommodate the species with the largest area requirement. Second, the larger the area, the higher the probability that it includes different habitats within it. A block of grass several hundred acres in size may have some wetlands, a hilltop with shorter grasses, some shrubs, and so forth. A five-acre block of habitat won't have much variation.

Large blocks of habitat also help protect against predation. Finding a nest in a large patch of grass is harder than finding a nest in a small patch of grass. Sovada et al. (2000) found that daily survival rates of waterfowl nests were greater in larger patches of grassland habitat. In another study, Phillips et al. (2003) found that red fox predation rates in the centers of large blocks of grass were lower than they were on the edges of these blocks or in small blocks.

The last benefit of large blocks of habitat is that there are more options for managing the habitat within each block. It is challenging to have multiple simultaneous uses on a 40-acre patch of grass. On a 400- or 4,000-acre tract of habitat this becomes much easier. Part of the area is hayed, part is grazed early in the summer, part is grazed later in the summer, some of the area is burned, some areas may be harvested for prairie seed, and some part of the grass will be rested. Within that one block of habitat, prairie-chickens can find every habitat type they need over the entire year.

Prairie-chickens probably do need a few large blocks of grassland, on the order of several thousand acres each, on the landscape. However, they don't just need those very large blocks. They can get by with smaller blocks scattered around these larger areas. In a Minnesota study, prairie-chickens were not detected in any grassland area smaller than 350 acres (Winter, Johnson, and Shaffer 2006). Researchers in Missouri (Ryan, Burger, and Jones 1998) recommended blocks of prairie-chicken habitat of 160 acres or more, as these offer the best potential for prairie-chicken conservation. In Illinois, Walk and Warner (1999) stated that the minimum area requirement for prairie-chickens was about 160 acres. In another Missouri study, prairie-chickens were not found in any grassland smaller than 320 acres (Winter and Faaborg 1999). My own observations of prairie-chickens in northwest Minnesota point to 320 acres as the minimum size of grassland habitat that prairie-chickens will use. This is a convenient number, as 320 acres is half a section, or half a square mile. This coincidentally reinforces historical references that prairie-chickens were most abundant when the landscape was half grass and half row crops.

Large blocks of habitat provide core areas for prairie-chicken populations. What they need is a few of these large blocks but with the smaller 160- to 320-acre patches scattered around and between them. This allows prairie-chickens to expand their population over a larger regional area. It also allows birds, and their genes, to move from one large block of habitat to another.

Probably no one bird will travel hundreds of miles. But a bird could fly from one large block and breed with other birds, and their offspring could continue moving to the next large block. In this way, birds and their genes can move across large regions.

The Midwest was broken into pieces of 40, 80, 160, and 640 acres before it was settled. Within any square mile, there are often several landowners. The number of landowners rises rapidly as the size of the area increases. Any large-scale or regional management plan in the Midwest covers the properties of hundreds of individual farmers and ranchers.

In my own township, there are five or six booming grounds. Each booming ground is on a different person's property. There is one flock that I watch each winter. Over the course of the year I see birds from that flock on at least five different properties. This is different from western rangelands, where the federal or state government can own large tracts of land such as national forests or national grasslands covering thousands of acres.

The practical realities of life are that the conservation community will never have the finances and the Midwest will never have the political or economic will to retire contiguous blocks of habitat covering thousands of acres. It has happened in a few areas, but those are the exceptions, not the rule.

Managers usually don't say that we have to buy and restore to prairie *that* piece of land to protect grassland birds. If that landowner doesn't want to do some habitat restoration, maybe a neighbor will. What is relevant for grassland birds is the density of grass at a slightly larger scale, for instance, the six-by-six-mile area defined by a township. Nesting success starts to improve when a certain percentage of the landscape is grass. It doesn't matter whether a particular parcel of land is grass, as long as there is a reasonable amount of grass in the general area (Walker et al. 2013).

Typically, wildlife managers and ecologists talk about habitat fragmentation as being negative. However, there are upsides to habitat fragmentation, depending on the scale at which you study the issue. Hamerstrom, Mattson, and Hamerstrom (1957) developed an early landscape-level plan for prairie-chicken management, which they called ecological patterning. Their idea was to place 40 acres of grass into every section, or square mile. A section is 640 acres. Today's research tells us that the patches need to be bigger than 40 acres, but the principle still applies.

This checkerboard pattern scatters habitat over a large area. Now, the eggs are in many different baskets. If there's a wildfire in one area during the nesting season, other areas won't be affected. It can be easier to manage a series of smaller blocks. Every year 25 percent of all the blocks in an area could be burned. One block could be hayed, the adjacent block could be rested, and the block on the next section could be grazed.

One way this idea has been formalized is with Grassland Bird Conservation Areas (GBCAs). The US Fish and Wildlife Service defines three sizes of GBCAs. The core areas of contiguous grass are 640, 160, and 55 acres in size, with a certain percentage of buffer area around the core also in grass. However, for a bird as large as the prairie-chicken, it would take a number of these GBCAs scattered over a landscape to support a sustainable population.

It's not enough to have just acres of habitat. Quality is just as important as quantity. One way to measure quality is by food availability. High plant diversity will produce a wider range of fruits and seeds for birds to eat. Perhaps more importantly, more plant species will attract more pollinating and herbivorous insects (Symstad, Siemann, and Haarstad 2000; Hines and Hendrix 2005). These will in turn attract more predatory insects. As insects are the primary food for egg-laying hens and growing chicks (Hill 1985; Whitmore, Pruess, and Gold 1986; Doxon and Carroll 2010), the more insects within the habitat, the better. Working with lesser prairie-chickens, Hagen et al. (2005) did find a correlation between areas with higher brood use and high insect density. Working with prairie-chickens in Minnesota, Syrowitz (2013) found a correlation between insect density and brood survival. One of the best ways to promote plant and insect diversity and abundance is through ecological disturbances such as fire, grazing, or haying.

Prairie-chickens are birds of working lands. The opening paragraph of this chapter cited papers with the words "land use" in them. The lands are used; they are part of the agricultural economy. They just need to be used in a sustainable manner. The birds don't need habitat that is set aside or locked up. They do just fine with grass that is hayed or grazed, just not too much. During the settlement period in Iowa, prairie-chickens thrived in this agricultural landscape.

The early settlement pattern created a landscape checkered by numerous small fields of various grain crops, hayfields, pastures, and remnant stands of native prairie. This landscape probably provided ideal prairie-chicken habitat, including food, winter and nesting cover, and exposed areas where males gathered to display to females. (Dinsmore 1994)

Granted, too much of a good thing (overgrazing) can be detrimental, but overall these birds do best in agriculturally productive grasslands.

Grazing provides several benefits. It increases plant diversity and can also increase invertebrate abundance (Joern 2005). It also has an important influence on the structural diversity of the vegetation for broods. A solid mass of ungrazed grass can be difficult for people to walk through. Imagine being a chick that weighs practically nothing. Grazed grass creates good foraging habitat, allowing chicks to move around with ease. What's important is that there is always a clump of taller vegetation nearby in case a raptor flies over or there's a sudden rainstorm. In addition, if you've ever walked in the morning prairie, you know that your pants are usually soaked within a few steps from all the dew on the blades of grass. It's often pretty chilly also. Again, imagine how cold it would be for a tiny chick. Grazing creates open areas where chicks can get away from the dew and into the morning sun to warm themselves.

These haymeadow days were Arcadian age for marsh dwellers. Man and beast, plant and soil lived on and with each other in mutual toleration, to the mutual benefit of all. The marsh might have kept on producing hay and prairie chickens, deer and muskrat, crane-music and cranberries forever. (Leopold 1949)

That these birds can maintain themselves in good numbers in close contact with certain types of agriculture must be regarded as a highly encouraging sign. (Yeatter 1943)

Next to lumbering and fire, agriculture was the most important factor in the past history of the prairie grouse in Michigan. It was an improvement in some areas over the "wild" habitat for prairie chickens. Small grains increased the quality and amount of available food and may have been a critical item under certain conditions in some areas. Forage crops provide good cover where such was scarce or lacking, and pastures, stubble fields, and mowed hayfields all increased the value of the habitat for prairie chickens by providing a variety of cover types. (Ammann 1957)

Farming practices largely explain why prairie-chickens followed the plow as settlers moved west and north across the Midwest, Great Plains, and Prairie Provinces.

What about hay meadows? Isn't a partly hayed country more favorable to prairie chickens than one left entirely uncut? (Leopold 1999)

Prairie chickens are benefited by moderate grazing of pastures. The paths and small areas of reduced cover resulting from the activities of the cattle facilitate the movements of young birds, and provide places suitable for sunning in times when the grass is wet. (Baker 1953)

A Kansas biologist, Gerald Horak, who has studied the birds in Chase County, believes the grouse declined after the bison were driven from the tall prairies because it depends on seasonal grazing to open up the grass. (Least Heat-Moon 1991)

Svedarsky (1988) reported that disturbed areas accounted for 70 percent of brood locations early in the summer and 80 percent of brood locations late in the summer. Prairie-chicken management is perfectly compatible with agricultural practices, if they are done with wildlife populations in mind.

Our analyses suggest that inadequate interspersion of open areas within the grassland structure may have contributed to population declines in recent years. Given that grazing is used as a tool to increase habitat heterogeneity for prairie-chickens (U.S. Fish and Wildlife

Service 1993), insufficient grazing may have resulted in this condition. (Morrow et al. 1996)

Ranchers, their hay mowers, and their cattle can be good friends to prairie wildlife. Across the prairies, livestock and the ranching economy are hurting almost as much as the wildlife. Historically, conservationists have pointed a lot of fingers at ranchers and their cows. And sometimes that is justified. However, both livestock and grassland birds need one thing above all else: grass. In this way, they should be the best of friends.

People often equate grazing with overgrazing. A good rancher follows the old adage of "take half, leave half." This ensures that the plants will remain healthy and strong the following year. With this philosophy there will be plenty of cover for wildlife throughout the year. Stohlgren (2000) wrote an article in *Nature Conservancy Magazine* titled "Good Cow, Bad Cow." When used with wildlife in mind, grazers can be excellent habitat management tools. When abused, they can be quite destructive of habitat.

Many people want to graze with bison, as they are more natural than cattle. Yes, but no. It's the management, not the grazing animal. "We found that plant communities in bison-grazed and cattle-grazed pastures were relatively similar through time, suggesting that the differences in how the herbivores are managed may play a larger role in their impact on prairie vegetation than differences between species" (Towne, Hartnett, and Cochran 2005). Within a twenty-minute drive from my house, there is a well-managed cattle pasture that is teeming with wildflowers, songbirds, and prairie-chickens. Another area grazed by bison makes the surface of the moon look like a tropical rain forest. The difference is management.

Traditionally, agriculture tries to homogenize the landscape. Farmers use lasers to level their fields and apply fertilizers to the soil so that every corn plant across the entire field will be the same size. Ranchers place stock ponds strategically across pastures to try to get livestock to spread out and evenly utilize the forage. However, researchers in Oklahoma have made good arguments that we should manage our grassland for heterogeneity (Coppedge et al. 2008). Every species of wildlife will find ideal habitat somewhere in that matrix of shorter and taller vegetation. "This evaluation of the functionality of heterogeneity in tallgrass prairie indicates the potential of using heterogeneity to integrate conservation biology and production agriculture on native grasslands" (Fuhlendorf and Engle 2004).

Mallards like to nest in tall, dense grass. Marbled godwits and upland sandpipers prefer very short grass. Prairie-chickens need all types over the season. In the spring, they need short grass for their booming ground. Later, they need taller grass for nesting. In the summer, they like patchy grazed grass for brood rearing.

Too many of our conservation grasslands in the Midwest are tall, thick, and undisturbed. In parts of the prairie region where there is little prairie in small fragments, such as Indiana and Illinois, we probably do need to manage these areas more as gardens than as functioning ecosystems. However, where there are larger tracts of grass or numerous tracts within a relatively short distance of each other, it would be beneficial to many wildlife species to actively manage these areas.

One of the best ways to manage for heterogeneity is with cattle grazing. A relatively new method for managing livestock is patch burn grazing. This method combines the two ecological disturbances that prairie plants and wildlife evolved under: fire and grazing. Only one perimeter fence is needed around the edge of the pasture. Given the numbers of prairie-chickens that are killed flying into fences, any cross-fencing or internal fencing we can eliminate within a grassland will be beneficial. Each spring, ranchers burn about a quarter of the pasture. The cattle are attracted to the vigorously growing vegetation in the freshly burned area and will stay in this area all summer. By fall, that area will be heavily grazed. Because they are so strongly attracted to that area, the cattle will have minimal impact on the other three-quarters of the pasture.

Next spring, ranchers burn another quarter. The cattle move over there. The birds—all birds—still have half the pasture with good nesting cover. The quarter the cattle grazed last year will probably have some annual weeds in it because of the disturbance. Annual weeds attract insects and produce lots of big seeds. The burned area is a good place for booming males, the unburned area provides good nesting and roosting cover, and the area recently burned and grazed will be very good for raising broods of chicks. This meets all the needs of prairie-chickens over the entire year within the same grassland patch.

Now, imagine if a number of ranchers were all doing this. There would be not only heterogeneity within each pasture, but heterogeneity between adjacent pastures. Anecdotally, the ranchers who have tried this method have been very happy with it. Because the grass has been rested for at least a couple of years, it is very nutritious. Cattle come off the prairie in the fall fat and healthy.

In the area of grassland bird conservation, the prairie-chicken can serve as an umbrella species for all midwestern grassland-nesting birds (Poiani, Merrill, and Chapman 2001). Of all the grassland-nesting birds, prairie-chickens require the most grass and the greatest diversity of grassland habitats and range of management. There are dozens of other grassland birds and other species of plants and wildlife that share these same habitats. Instead of managing for each of these dozens of species, we can manage for prairie-chickens and by default cover almost all of the other species that occupy midwestern grasslands.

Many look to the government to solve wildlife problems. But in the midwestern prairie landscape where prairie-chickens lived and still live, the vast majority of the land is in private ownership. It's the actions of individual farmers, ranchers, conservationists, and citizens that will determine the fate of prairie-chickens and other tallgrass prairie birds.

The future of the prairie chicken is in the hands of the landowners of America. (W. Grange 1939)

We've been studying prairie-chickens and other grassland birds for decades now. You'd think we'd know what we were doing. But as with life in general, we often have as many questions as answers. "Managers need to be willing to admit uncertainty in dealing with constituents. . . . We should be willing to say 'We just don't know'" (Applegate, Williams, and Manes 2004).

Indeed, any good research project should answer a few questions and bring up many more. This is often frustrating to the general public, who want concrete answers in short sound bites. Prairie-chickens are complex creatures living in very dynamic landscapes. There are still many unanswered questions and much research yet to be done. We all need to humbly admit that the prairie is a vast, complex system, and we've only scratched the surface. But there is one thing we know with certainty.

Wherever one looks, the answer is the same: to save the prairie chicken, grasslands must be preserved and managed for them. There are no substitutes. (Hamerstrom, Mattson, and Hamerstrom 1957)

Simply put, prairie grouse require prairie and lots of it. (Silvy, Peterson, and Lopez 2004)

It really shouldn't be that hard to save this species. Large carnivores do need vast tracts of wilderness devoid of human presence. That's really the only way we can save some of them. As unpopular as this might be among many people, we do need to lock up land for these species. Many other species are absolutely intolerant of human presence and they need a place, usually a big place, where we humans aren't. Not so with the prairie-chicken.

Wildlife management and conservation are both incredibly complex and very simple. The details are complex. The generalities are simple. Grassland wildlife needs grass.

Conclusion

Joy cometh in the morning. —*Psalms 30:5*

Within the Midwest, if there are healthy, productive grasslands in large enough blocks scattered over the regional landscape, there will be prairie-chickens. Without grassland, there will be no prairie-chickens and few other grassland birds.

While government agencies such as the US Fish and Wildlife Service, each state's Department of Natural Resources, and nongovernmental organizations such as the Nature Conservancy can be major players in the future of the prairie-chicken and other prairie wildlife, the true fate of all these species lies in the hands of farmers, ranchers, and rural landowners.

Recent years have not been good for prairie lovers. Conservation Reserve Program acres and other grasslands have been plowed up at almost unprecedented rates. Agricultural policies as well as new technologies have encouraged the plowing up of the last remaining native prairies, and the highest, driest, and rockiest as well as the lowest, wettest, and muckiest prairies are disappearing. It's not a fun time to drive around the Midwest. Aldo Leopold said that the tragedy of an ecological education is that you live in a world of wounds. There is no more wounded landscape on the American continent than our grasslands.

Many of us are often a little down and crabby by late March, our mood correlated to the temperatures and the snow shoveled over the past couple of months. But then there are April mornings on the Agassiz Beach Ridges of northwest Minnesota, the Sand Hills of Nebraska, the Flint and Osage Hills of Kansas and Oklahoma, and a few other areas. T. S. Eliot said that April was the cruelest month. Mr. Eliot never watched prairie-chickens as the cold April sun crested the horizon.

Frederick Hamerstrom once famously said that the good deeds of conservation do not need to be done in a sepulchral atmosphere. All too often, it's easy to get down when discussing conservation issues in the Midwest. Here I stand on a cold April morning in a devastated landscape watching a glorious display, caught between the ideas of Leopold and Hamerstrom. But if you ever need an uplifting experience, a sense of renewal, and a way to recharge your batteries, spend a morning watching prairie-chickens booming from the mists of nowhere. It's impossible not to be inspired and energized by the time you leave. If there's a pasqueflower hugging the frozen ground at your feet, all the better.

When winter clouds lower and the brown prairies swirl to the anger of the sullen prairie winds, to see and hear the flutter and wings of a flock of prairie chickens is to have brown prairies slip the leash of the earth and take to the sky. (Quayle 1925)

Bibliography

Ammann, G. A. 1957. *The Prairie Grouse of Michigan*. Lansing, MI: Department of Conservation.

Applegate, R. D., C. K. Williams, and R. R. Manes. 2004. "Assuring the Future of Prairie Grouse: Dogmas, Demagogues, and Getting Outside the Box." *Wildlife Society Bulletin* 32(1): 104–11.

Archer, S., and C. Bunch. 1953. *American Grass Book: A Manual of Pasture and Range Practices*. Norman: University of Oklahoma Press.

Arthaud, F. L. 1970. "Land Use and Prairie Chicken Populations in Southwestern Missouri." *Transactions of the Kansas Academy of Science* 73(2): 267–76.

Askins, C. 1931. *Game Bird Shooting*. New York: Macmillan.

Audubon, J. J. 1831. *Birds of America*. Philadelphia: Judah Dobson.

Bakeless, J. 1950. *America as Seen by Its First Explorers: The Eyes to Discovery*. Toronto: General Publishing.

Baker, M. F. 1953. *Prairie Chickens of Kansas*. Lawrence: State Biological Survey, University of Kansas.

Ballard, W. B., and R. J. Robel. 1974. "Reproductive Importance of Dominant Male Greater Prairie Chickens." *Auk* 91:75–85.

Bateson, Z. W., P. O. Dunn, S. D. Hull, A. E. Henschen, J. A. Johnson, and L. A. Whittingham. 2014. "Genetic Restoration of a Threatened Population of Greater Prairie-Chickens." *Biological Conservation* 174:12–19.

Beck, J. V. 1957. "The Greater Prairie Chicken in History." *Nebraska Bird Review* 25:8–12.

Bellinger, M. R., J. A. Johnson, J. Toepfer, and P. Dunn. 2003. "Loss of Genetic Variation in Greater Prairie Chickens following a Population Bottleneck in Wisconsin, U.S.A." *Conservation Biology* 17(3): 717–24.

Bent, A. C. 1932. *Life Histories of North American Gallinaceous Birds*. Smithsonian Institution United States National Museum Bulletin 162.

Berg, W. E. 2004. "Epilogue: The Ghosts of Prairie Grouse Past." *Wildlife Society Bulletin* 32(1): 123–26.

Bergerud, A. T., and M. W. Gratson, eds. 1988. *Adaptive Strategies and Population Ecology of Northern Grouse*. Vols. 1 and 2. Saint Paul: University of Minnesota Press.

Betten, H. L. 1940. *Upland Game Shooting*. New York: Alfred Knopf.

Blus, L. J., and J. A. Walker. 1966. "Progress Report on the Prairie Grouse Nesting Study in the Nebraska Sandhills." *Nebraska Bird Review* 34:23–30.

Boatman, N., N. Brickle, J. Hart, T. Milsom, A. Morris, A. Murray, K. Murray, and P. Robertson. 2004. "Evidence for the Indirect Effects of Pesticides on Farmland Birds." *Ibis* 146 (supplement s2): 131–43.

Bogardus, A. H. 1878. *Field, Cover, and Trap Shooting*. Prescott, AZ: Wolf Publishing.

Bouzat, J. L. 2010. "Conservation Genetics of Population Bottlenecks: The Role of Chance, Selection, and History." *Conservation Genetics* 11:463–78.

Bouzat, J. L., H. H. Cheng, H. A. Lewin, R. L. Westemeier, J. D. Brawn, and K. N. Paige. 1998. "Genetic Evaluation of a Demographic Bottleneck in the Greater Prairie Chicken." *Conservation Biology* 12(4): 836–43.

Bouzat, J. L., J. A. Johnson, J. E. Toepfer, S. A. Simpson, T. L. Esker, and R. L. Westemeier. 2009. "Beyond the Beneficial Effects of Translocations as an Effective Tool for the Genetic Restoration of Isolated Populations." *Conservation Genetics* 10:191–201.

Bouzat, J. L., H. A. Lewin, and K. N. Paige. 1998. "The Ghost of Genetic Diversity Past: Historical DNA Analysis of the Greater Prairie Chicken." *American Naturalist* 152(1): 1–6.

Bradbury, J. W. 1981. "The Evolution of Leks." In *Natural Selection and Social Behavior*, edited by R. D. Alexander and D. W. Winkle, 138–69. New York: Chiron Press.

Briggs, J., and A. Knapp. 1995. "Interannual Variability in Primary Production in Tallgrass Prairie: Climate, Soil Moisture, Topographic Position, and Fire as Determinants of Aboveground Biomass." *American Journal of Botany* 82:1024–30.

Bruette, W. 1916. "Season of the Prairie Chicken." *Forest and Stream* 86(8): 1079–81, 1116.

Cather, W. 1918. *My Antonia*. Boston: Houghton Mifflin.

Changnon, S. A., K. E. Kunkel, and D. Winstanley. 2003. "Quantification of

Climate Conditions Important to the Tall Grass Prairie." *Transactions of the Illinois State Academy of Science* 96(1): 41–54.

Chapman, F. 1908. *Camps and Cruises of an Ornithologist*. New York: D. Appleton.

Christisen, D. M. 1969. "National Status and Management of the Greater Prairie Chicken." *Thirty-Fourth North American Wildlife Conference* 34:207–17.

———. 1981. "Significance of Native Prairie to Greater Prairie Chicken (*Tympanuchus cupido pinnatus*) Survival in Missouri." *Ohio Biological Survey, Biological Notes*, no. 15: 250–54.

Coppedge, B. R., S. D. Fuhlendorf, W. C. Harrell, and D. M. Engle. 2008. "Avian Community Response to Vegetation and Structural Features in Grasslands Managed with Fire and Grazing." *Biological Conservation* 141:1196–1203.

Courtwright, J. 2011. *Prairie Fire: A Great Plains History*. Lawrence: University Press of Kansas.

Curtis, P. A. 1930. "Prairie Chicken Shooting." In *Upland Game Bird Shooting in America*, edited by E. V. Connett, 73–80. Lyon, MS: Derrydale Press.

Dalrymple, B. W. 1950. "Has the Prairie Chicken a Future?" *Sports Afield*, August, 19–21, 74–77.

Darwin, C. 1871. *The Descent of Man and Selection in Relation to Sex*. London: John Murray.

Davis, T. 2004. *The Tattered Autumn Sky: Bird Hunting in the Heartland*. Guilford, CT: Lyons Press.

Dinsmore, J. J. 1994. *A Country So Full of Game: The History of Wildlife in Iowa*. Iowa City: University of Iowa Press.

Doxon, E. D., and J. P. Carroll. 2010. "Feeding Ecology of Ring-Necked Pheasant and Northern Bobwhite Chicks in Conservation Reserve Program Fields." *Journal of Wildlife Management* 74(2): 249–56.

Drobney, R. D., and R. D. Sparrowe. 1977. "Land Use Relationships and Movements of Greater Prairie Chickens in Missouri." *Transactions of the Missouri Academy of Science* 10 and 11:146–60.

Duebbert, H. F. 2003. *Wildfowling in Dakota, 1873–1903*. Bismarck, ND: Windfeather Press.

Duebbert, H., and H. Kantrud. 1974. "Upland Duck Nesting Related to Land Use and Predator Reduction." *Journal of Wildlife Management* 38:257–65.

Duebbert, H., and J. Lokemoen. 1980. "High Duck Nesting Success in a Predator-Reduced Environment." *Journal of Wildlife Management* 44:428–37.

Edmands, S. 2007. "Between a Rock and a Hard Place: Evaluating the Relative Risks of Inbreeding and Outbreeding for Conservation and Management." *Molecular Ecology* 16:463–75.

Elliott, C. 1974. *Prince of Game Birds: The Bobwhite Quail*. Georgia Department of Natural Resources.

Ernst, F. 1903. "Observations Made upon a Journey through the Interior of the United States of North America in the Year 1819." Translated by E. P. Baker. *Transactions of the Illinois State Historical Society* 8(1903): 150–165. First published 1823 in Hildesheim, Germany.

Errington, P. L. 1987. *A Question of Values*. Ames: Iowa State University Press.

Esten, S. R. 1933. "Notes on the Prairie Chicken in Indiana." *Auk* 50(3): 356–57.

European Food Safety Authority. 2013. "Scientific Opinion on the Developmental Neurotoxicity Potential of Acetamiprid and Imidacloprid." *EFSA Journal* 11(12): 1–20.

Faragher, J. M. 1986. *Sugar Creek: Life on the Illinois Prairie*. New Haven, CT: Yale University Press.

Farnham, E.W. 1988. *Life in Prairie Land*. Urbana: University of Illinois Press.

Farrar, J. 1980. "In Quest of the Prairie Hen." *Nebraskaland*, September, 12–15, 42–46.

Featherstonhaugh, G. W. 1847. *A Canoe Voyage up the Minnay Sotor*. London: Richard Bentley.

Fergus, J. 1999. "Of Flushing Mules and Prairie Tuna." In *The Sporting Road*, 78–86. New York: St. Martin's Press.

Fishel, F. M. 2013. *Pesticide Toxicity Profile: Neonicotinoid Pesticides*. University of Florida Extension, PI-80.

Flanders-Wanner, B. L., G. C. White, and L. L. McDaniel. 2004. "Weather and Prairie Grouse: Dealing with Effects beyond Our Control." *Wildlife Society Bulletin* 32(1): 22–34.

Fleharty, E. D. 1995. *Wild Animals and Settlers on the Great Plains*. Norman: University of Oklahoma Press.

Forester, F. 1866. "Grouse-Shooting on the Prairies." In *The Complete Manual for Young Sportsmen*, 296–305. New York: Arno Press.

Franklin, I. 1980. "Evolutionary Changes in Small Populations." In *Conservation Biology: An Evolutionary-Ecological Perspective*, edited by M. Soule and B. Wilcox, 135–49. Sunderland, MA: Sinauer.

Franklin, I., and R. Frankham. 1998. "How Large Must Populations Be to Retain Evolutionary Potential?" *Animal Conservation* 1:69–73.

Fuhlendorf, S., and D. Engle. 2004. "Application of the Fire-Grazing Interaction to Restore a Shifting Mosaic on Tallgrass Prairie." *Journal of Applied Ecology* 41(4): 604–14.

Garland, H. 1917. *Son of the Middle Border*. New York: Grosset and Dunlap.

Gibbons, D., C. Morrissey, and P. Mineau. 2014. "A Review of the Direct and Indirect Effects of Neonicotinoids and Fipronil on Vertebrate Wildlife." *Environmental Science and Pollution Research* 22(1): 103–18, doi:10.1007 /s11356-014-3180-5.

Gillmore, P. 1874. "Grouse." In *Prairie and Forest: A Description of the Game of North America*, 193–209. New York: Harper and Brothers.

Goulson, D. 2013. "An Overview of the Environmental Risks Posed by Neonicotinoid Insecticides." *Journal of Applied Ecology* 50:977–87.

Grange, H. 1996. *Live Arrival Guaranteed: A Sandhill Memoir*. Boulder Junction, WI: Lost River Press.

Grange, W. B. 1939. "Can We Preserve the Prairie Chicken?" *Game Breeder and Sportsman*, April, 58–59, 62–63.

———. 1948. *Wisconsin Grouse Problems*. Madison: Wisconsin Conservation Department.

Greenberg, J. 2002. *A Natural History of the Chicago Region*. Chicago: University of Chicago Press.

Grinnell, G. B. 1910. *American Game Bird Shooting*. New York: Forest and Stream Publishing.

Gross, A. O. 1930. *Progress Report of the Wisconsin Prairie Chicken Investigation*. Madison: Wisconsin Conservation Commission.

H., W. R. 1894. "About Prairie Chicken Trapping." *Forest and Stream* 43(26): 560.

Hagen, C. A., G. C. Salter, J. C. Pitman, R. J. Robel, and R. D. Applegate. 2005. "Lesser Prairie-Chicken Brood Habitat in Sand Sagebrush: Invertebrate Biomass and Vegetation." *Wildlife Society Bulletin* 33(3): 1080–91.

Plumbe, J., Jr. 1839. *Sketches of Iowa and Wisconsin, Taken during a Residence of Three Years in Those Territories*. Saint Louis: Chambers, Harris, and Knapp.

Hamerstrom, F. 1980. *Strictly for the Chickens*. Ames: Iowa State University Press.

———. 1989. *Is She Coming Too? Memoirs of a Lady Hunter*. Ames: Iowa State University Press.

Hamerstrom, F., and F. Hamerstrom. 1973. *The Prairie Chicken in Wisconsin: Highlights of a 22-Year Study of Counts, Behavior, Movements, Turnover, and Habitat*. Technical Bulletin No. 64. Wisconsin Department of Natural Resources.

Hamerstrom, F. N. 1939. "A Study of Wisconsin Prairie Chicken and Sharp-Tailed Grouse." *Wilson Bulletin* 51(2): 105–20.

Hamerstrom, F. N., and F. Hamerstrom. 1949. "Daily and Seasonal Movements of Wisconsin Prairie Chickens." *Auk* 66:313–37.

Hamerstrom, F. N., O. E. Mattson, and F. Hamerstrom. 1957. *A Guide to Prairie Chicken Management*. Technical Wildlife Bulletin No. 15. Wisconsin Conservation Department.

Hamilton, W. D., and M. Zuk. 1982. "Heritable True Fitness and Bright Birds: A Role for Parasites?" *Science* 218:384–87.

Harrison, R. 1974. "Memoirs of the Prairie Chicken." *Kansas Game and Fish* 31(5): 11–14.

Helzer, C. J., and D. E. Zelinski. 1999. "The Relative Importance of Patch Area and Perimeter-Area Ratio to Grassland Breeding Birds." *Ecological Applications* 9(4): 1448–58.

Herkert, J. R. 1994. "The Effects of Habitat Fragmentation on Midwestern Grassland Bird Communities." *Ecological Applications* 4(3): 461–71.

Hickman, K. R., D. C. Hartnett, R. C. Cochran, and C. E. Owensby. 2004. "Grazing Management Effects on Plant Species Diversity in Tallgrass Prairie." *Journal of Range Management* 57(1): 58–65.

Hill, D. A. 1985. "The Feeding Ecology and Survival of Pheasant Chicks on Arable Farmland." *Journal of Applied Ecology* 22:645–54.

Hines, H., and S. Hendrix. 2005. "Bumble Bee (Hymenoptera: Apidae) Diversity and Abundance in Tallgrass Prairie Patches: Effects of Local and Landscape Floral Resources." *Environmental Entomology* 34(6): 1477–84.

Hladik, M. L., D. W. Kolpin, and K. Kuivila. 2014. "Widespread Occurrence of Neonicotinoid Insecticides in Streams in a High Corn and Soybean Producing Region, USA." *Environmental Pollution* 193:189–96.

Hoglund, J., and R. V. Alatalo. 1995. *Leks*. Princeton, NJ: Princeton University Press.

Hopwood, J., S. Black, M. Vaughan, and E. Mader. 2013. *Beyond the Birds and the Bees: The Effects of Neonicotinoid Insecticides on Agriculturally Important Beneficial Invertebrates*. Portland, OR: Xerces Society for Invertebrate Conservation.

Horak, G. J. 1985. *Kansas Prairie Chickens*. Wildlife Bulletin 3. Pratt: Kansas Game and Fish Commission.

Hornaday, W. T. 1904. *Hornaday's American Natural History*. New York: Charles Scribner's Sons.

Hough, H. B. 1933. *The Heath Hen's Journey to Extinction, 1792–1933*. Edgartown, MA: Dukes County Historical Society.

Houston, C. S. 2002. "Spread and Disappearance of the Greater Prairie-Chicken, *Tympanuchus cupido*, on the Canadian Prairies and Adjacent Areas." *Canadian Field-Naturalist* 116(1): 1–21.

Huntington, D. W. 1903. "The Prairie Grouse." In *Our Feathered Game*, 65–72. New York: Charles Scribner's Sons.

Irvine, P. 1935. "Prairie Chickens in Duck Weather." *Outdoor Life*, October, 16–17, 59.

Irving, W. 1956. *A Tour on the Prairies*. Norman: University of Oklahoma Press.

Joern, A. 2005. "Disturbance by Fire Frequency and Bison Grazing Modulate Grasshopper Assemblages in Tallgrass Prairie." *Ecology* 86(4): 861–73.

Johnsgard, P. A. 1983. *The Grouse of the World*. Lincoln: University of Nebraska Press.

——. 2002. *Grassland Grouse and Their Conservation*. Washington, DC: Smithsonian Institution Press.

——. 2003. *Great Wildlife of the Great Plains*. Lawrence: University Press of Kansas.

——. 2014. *Seasons of the Tallgrass Prairie*. Lincoln: University of Nebraska Press.

Johnsgard, P. A., and R. E. Wood. 1968. "Distributional Changes and Interaction between Prairie Chickens and Sharp-Tailed Grouse in the Midwest." *Wilson Bulletin* 80(2): 173–88.

Johnson, C. E. 1934. "Recollections of the Prairie Chicken and Sharp-Tailed Grouse in Northwestern Minnesota." *Wilson Bulletin* 47(1): 3–17.

Johnson, G. D., W. P. Erickson, M. D. Strickland, M. F. Shepherd, D. A. Shepherd, and S. A. Sapappo. 2002. "Collision Mortality of Local and Migrant Birds at a Large-Scale Wind-Power Development in Buffalo Ridge, Minnesota." *Wildlife Society Bulletin* 30(3): 879–87.

Johnson, J. A., M. R. Bellinger, J. E. Toepfer, and P. Dunn. 2004. "Temporal Changes in Allele Frequency and Low Effective Population Size in Greater Prairie-Chickens." *Molecular Ecology* 13:2617–30.

Johnson, J. A., and P. O. Dunn. 2006. "Low Genetic Variation in the Heath Hen Prior to Extinction and Implications for the Conservation of Prairie-Chicken Populations." *Conservation Genetics* 7:37–48.

Johnson, J. A., P. O. Dunn, and J. L. Bouzat. 2007. "Effects of Recent Population Bottlenecks on Reconstructing the Demographic History of Prairie-Chickens." *Molecular Ecology* 16:2203–22.

Johnson, J. A., J. E. Toepfer, and P. O. Dunn. 2003. "Contrasting Patterns of Mitochondrial and Microsatellite Population Structure in Fragmented

Populations of Greater Prairie-Chickens." *Molecular Ecology* 12:3335–47.

Johnson, M. D., and J. Knue. 1989. *Feathers from the Prairie*. Bismarck: North Dakota Game and Fish Department.

Jones, A., P. Harrington, and G. Turnbull. 2014. "Neonicotinoid Concentrations in Arable Soils after Seed Treatment Applications in Preceding Years." *Pest Management Science* 70(12): 1780–84.

Jones, R. E. 1963. "Identification and Analysis of Lesser and Greater Prairie Chicken Habitat." *Journal of Wildlife Management* 27(4): 757–78.

Jones, S. 1992. "After the Boom: The Demise of the Indiana Prairie Chicken." *Traces* 4(2): 38–47.

Kardash, L. H. 2008. *Central Wisconsin Greater Prairie-Chicken Survey*. Final Report. Wisconsin Department of Natural Resources.

Kimura-Kuroda, Y. Komuta, Y. Kuroda, M. Hayashi, and H. Kawano. 2012. "Nicotine-like Effects of the Neonicotinoid Insecticides Acetamiprid and Imidacloprid on Cerebellar Neurons from Neonatal Rats." *PLOS ONE* 7(2): e32432.

Kirsch, L. M. 1974. "Habitat Management Considerations for Prairie Chickens." *Wildlife Society Bulletin* 2(3): 124–29.

Kirsch, L. M., A. T. Klett, and H. W. Miller. 1973. "Land Use and Prairie Grouse Population Relationships in North Dakota." *Journal of Wildlife Management* 37(4): 449–453.

Klett, A., T. Shaffer, and D. Johnson. 1988. "Duck Nest Success in the Prairie Pothole Region." *Journal of Wildlife Management* 52(3): 431–40.

Kobriger, G. D. 1965. "Status, Movement, Habitats, and Foods of Prairie Grouse on a Sandhill Refuge." *Journal of Wildlife Management* 29(4): 788–800.

Kobriger, J. D., D. P. Vollink, M. E. Mcneill, and K. F. Higgins. 1987. "Prairie Chicken Populations of the Sheyenne Delta in North Dakota, 1961–1987." Prairie Chickens on the Sheyenne National Grassland Symposium, September 18, 1987, University of Minnesota, Crookston. Great Plains Agricultural Council Publication No. 123.

Korschgen, L. J. 1962. "Food Habits of Greater Prairie Chickens in Missouri." *American Midland Naturalist* 68(2): 307–18.

Kunkel, K. E., D. R. Easterling, K. Redmond, and K. Hubbard. 2003. "Temporal Variations of Extreme Precipitation Events in the United States: 1895–2000." *Geophysical Research Letters* 30:1900, doi:10.1029/2003GL018052.

Kunz, T. H., E. B. Arnett, W. P. Erickson, A. R. Hoar, G. D. Johnson, R. P. Larkin, M. D. Strickland, et al. 2007. "Ecological Impacts of Wind Energy Development on Bats: Questions, Research Needs, and Hypotheses." *Frontiers in Ecology and Environment* 5(6): 315–24.

Kuvlesky, W., L. Brennan, M. Morrison, K. Boydston, B. Ballard, and F. Bryant. 2007. "Wind Energy Development and Wildlife Conservation: Challenges and Opportunities." *Journal of Wildlife Management* 71(8): 2487–98.

Lande, R. 1995. "Mutation and Conservation." *Science* 241:1455–60.

Lande, R., and G. Barrowclough. 1987. "Effective Population Size, Genetic Variation, and Their Use in Population Management." In *Viable Populations for Conservation*, edited by M. Soule, 87–123. Cambridge: Cambridge University Press.

Laskin, D. 2004. *The Children's Blizzard*. New York: Harper Perennial.

Laycock, G. 1963. "The Prairie Chicken and His Friends." *Field and Stream*, September, 52–53, 86–89.

Least Heat-Moon, W. 1991. *PrairyErth*. Boston: Houghton Mifflin.

Leddy, K. L., K. F. Higgins, and D. E. Naugle. 1999. "Effects of Wind Turbines on Upland Nesting Birds in Conservation Reserve Program Grasslands." *Wilson Bulletin* 111(1): 100–104.

Leffingwell, W. B. 1890. "Prairie Chickens: Pinnated Grouse." In *Shooting on Upland, Marsh, and Stream*, edited by W. B. Leffingwell, 279–310. Chicago: Rand-McNally.

Leopold, A. 1931. *Report on a Game Survey of the North Central States*. Madison, WI: Sporting Arms and Ammunition Manufacturer's Association.

———. 1933. *Game Management*. New York: Charles Scribner's Sons.

———. 1949. *A Sand County Almanac*. New York: Oxford University Press.

———. 1991. *The River of the Mother of God and Other Essays*. Edited by S. F. Flader and J. B. Callicott. Madison: University of Wisconsin Press.

———. 1999. *For the Health of the Land: Previously Unpublished Essays and Other Writings*. Washington, DC: Island Press.

Lewis, E. 1863. "Pinnated Grouse, or Prairie Hen." In *The American Sportsman: Containing Hints to Sportsmen, Notes on Shooting, and the Habits of Game Birds and Wild Fowl of America*, 156–65. Philadelphia: Lippincott.

Ligon, J. S. 1951. "Prairie Chickens, Highways, and Power Lines." *New Mexico Magazine* 29(5): 29.

Lockart, J. 1960. "The Prairie Boomer." *Outdoors in Illinois* 7(2): 12–14.

Lowther, 1883. "Then and Now: The Extermination of Game." *American Field*, September 22, 269.

Lynch, M., and R. Lande. 1998. "The Critical Effective Size for a Genetically Secure Population." *Animal Conservation* 1(1): 70–72.

Madson, J. 1962. *The Ring-Necked Pheasant*. East Alton, IL: Conservation Department, Olin Mathieson Chemical Corporation.

———. 1979. *Out Home*. New York: Winchester Press.

———. 1982. *Where the Sky Began*. Iowa City: University of Iowa Press.

Main, A., J. Headley, K. Peru, N. Michel, A. Cessna, and C. Morrissey. 2014. "Widespread Use and Frequent Detection of Neonicotinoid Insecticides in Wetlands of Canada's Prairie Pothole Region." *PLOS ONE* 9(3): e92821.

Mason, R., H. Tennekes, F. Sanchez-Bayo, and P. Jepsen. 2012. Immune-Suppression by Neonicotinoid Insecticides at the Root of Global Wildlife Declines." *Journal of Environmental Immunology and Toxicology* 1(1): 3–12.

Matthews, T. W., A. J. Tyre, J. S. Taylor, J. J. Lusk, and L. A. Powell. 2013. "Greater Prairie-Chicken Nest Success and Habitat Selection in Southeastern Nebraska." *Journal of Wildlife Management* 77(6): 1202–12.

McClain, W. E., and S. L. Elzinga. 1994. "The Occurrence of Prairie and Forest Fires in Illinois and Other Midwestern States, 1670 to 1854." *Erigenia* 13:79–90.

McIntosh, M. 1997. *Traveler's Tales: The Wanderings of a Bird Hunter and Sometimes Fly Fisherman.* Camden, ME: Down East Books.

McKee, G., M. R. Ryan, and L. M. Mechlin. 1998. "Predicting Greater Prairie-Chicken Nest Success from Vegetation and Landscape Characteristics." *Journal of Wildlife Management* 62(1): 314–21.

McNew, L. B., A. J. Gregory, S. M. Wisely, and B. K. Sandercock. 2012. "Demography of Greater Prairie-Chickens: Regional Variation in Vital Rates, Sensitivity Values, and Population Dynamics." *Journal of Wildlife Management* 76(5): 987–1000.

Merrill, M. D., K. A. Chapman, K. A. Poiani, and B. Winter. 1999. "Land-Use Patterns Surrounding Greater Prairie-Chicken Leks in Northwestern Minnesota." *Journal of Wildlife Management* 63(1): 189–98.

Merritt, H. C. 1904. *The Shadow of a Gun.* Chicago: F. T. Peterson.

Mezquida, E. T., S. J. Slater, and C. W. Benkham. 2006. "Sage-Grouse and Indirect Interactions: Potential Implication of Coyote Control on Sage-Grouse Populations." *Condor* 108:747–59.

Mineau, P., and M. Whiteside. 2013. "Pesticide Acute Toxicity Is a Better Correlate of U.S. Grassland Bird Declines Than Agricultural Intensification." *PLOS ONE* 8(2): e57457.

Moe, M. 1999. "Status and Management of the Greater Prairie Chicken in Iowa." In *The Greater Prairie Chicken: A National Look*, 123–28. Minnesota Agricultural Experiment Station, Miscellaneous Publication 99-1999.

Morrow, M., R. Adamcik, J. Friday, and L. McKinney. 1996. "Factors Affecting Attwater's Prairie-Chicken Decline on the Attwater's Prairie Chicken National Wildlife Refuge." *Wildlife Society Bulletin* 24:593–601.

Morrow, M., T. Rossignol, J. E. Toepfer, and A. C. Pratt. 2010. "Attwater's Prairie Chicken Recovery: The Beginning or the End?" *Grouse Partnership News.*

Muir, J. 1913. *Story of My Boyhood and Youth*. San Francisco: Sierra Club Books.

Niemuth, N. D. 2000. "Land Use and Vegetation Associated with Greater Prairie-Chicken Leks in Agricultural Landscape." *Journal of Wildlife Management* 64(1): 278–86.

———. 2003. "Identifying Landscapes for Greater Prairie Chicken Translocations Using Habitat Models and GIS: A Case Study." *Wildlife Society Bulletin* 31(1): 145–55.

Nooker, J. K., and B. K. Sandercock. 2008. "Phenotypic Correlates and Survival Consequences of Male Mating Success in Lek-Mating Greater Prairie-Chickens (*Tympanuchus cupido*)." *Behavioral Ecology and Sociobiology* 62:1377–88.

O'Brien, D. 2001. *Buffalo for a Broken Heart: Restoring Life to a Black Hills Ranch*. New York: Random House.

Oliver, W. 1843. *Eight Months in Illinois*. W. A. Mitchell.

Osborn, R. G., K. F. Higgins, R. F. Usgaard, C. D. Dieter, and R. D. Neiger. 2000. "Bird Mortality Associated with Wind Turbines at the Buffalo Ridge Wind Resource Area, Minnesota." *American Midland Naturalist* 143:41–52.

Osborn, R. G, C. D. Sieter, K. F. Higgins, and R. E. Usgaard. 1998. "Bird Flight Characteristics near Wind Turbines in Minnesota." *American Midland Naturalist* 139:29–38.

Palliser, J. 1853. *Solitary Rambles and Adventures of a Hunter in the Prairies*. C. E. Tuttle, London.

Partch, M. 1970. "Prairie Chicken Exodus: Notes on the Prairie Chicken in Central Minnesota." *Loon* 42(1): 5–19.

Peattie, D. C. 1938. *A Prairie Grove*. New York: Literary Guild of America.

Peterson, M. J., and N. J. Silvy. 1996. "Reproductive Stages Limiting Productivity of the Endangered Attwater's Prairie Chicken." *Conservation Biology* 10:1264–76.

Phillips, M. L., W. R. Clark, M. A. Sovada, D. J. Horn, R. R. Koford, and R. J. Greenwood. 2003. "Predator Selection of Habitat Features in Prairie Landscapes with Contrasting Grassland Composition." *Journal of Wildlife Management* 67:104–14.

Pierce, F. J. 1922. "The Prairie Chicken in East Central Iowa." *Wilson Bulletin* 34(2): 100–106.

Pieron, M. R., and F. C. Rowher. 2010. "Effects of Large-Scale Predator Reduction on Nest Success of Upland Nesting Ducks." *Journal of Wildlife Management* 74:124–32.

Pitman, J., C. Hagen, R. Robel, T. Loughlin, and R. Applegate. 2005. "Location and Success of Lesser Prairie-Chicken Nests in Relation to Vegetation and Human Disturbance." *Journal of Wildlife Management* 69:1259–69.

Plumb, G., and J. Dodd. 1993. "Foraging Ecology of Bison and Cattle on a Mixed Prairie: Implications for Natural Areas Management." *Ecological Applications* 3(4): 631–43.

Poiani, K. A., M. D. Merrill, and K. A. Chapman. 2001. "Identifying Conservation Priority Areas in a Fragmented Minnesota Landscape Based on the Umbrella Species Concept and the Selection of Large Patches of Natural Vegetation." *Conservation Biology* 15(2): 513–22.

Potts, G. R. 2012. *Partridges*. London: Harper Collins.

"Prairie Chicken Shooting and Trapping Fifty Years Ago." 1883. *American Field*, December 1, 807.

Pruett, C. L., M. A. Patten, and D. H. Wolfe. 2009. "Avoidance Behavior by Prairie Grouse: Implications for Development of Wind Energy." *Conservation Biology* 23(5): 1253–59.

Pyne, S. J. 1982. *Fire in America: A Cultural History of Wildland and Rural Fire*. Princeton, NJ: Princeton University Press.

Quayle, W. A. 1905. *The Prairie and the Sea*. Cincinnati: Jennings and Graham.

Quick, H. 1925. *One Man's Life*. Brooklyn, NY: Braunworth.

Ripley, O. 1926. "Prairie Chicken." In *Sport in Field and Forest*, 127–38. New York: D. Appleton.

Robel, R. J. 1967. "Significance of Booming Ground of Greater Prairie Chickens." *Proceedings of the American Philosophical Society* 111(2): 109–14.

Robel, R. J., J. N. Briggs, J. J. Cebula, N. J. Silvy, C. E. Viers, and P. G. Watts. 1970. "Greater Prairie Chicken Ranges, Movements, and Habitat Usage in Kansas." *Journal of Wildlife Management* 43(2): 286–306.

Robel, R. J., J. A. Harrington, C. A. Hagen, J. C. Pitman, and R. R. Recker. 2004. "Effect of Energy Development and Human Activity on the Use of Sand Sagebrush Habitat by Lesser Prairie-Chickens in Southwestern Kansas." *Transactions of the North American Natural Resources Conference* 69:251–66.

Roosevelt, T. 1899. *Hunting Trips of a Ranchman*. New York: Putnam's Sons.

Ryan, M. R., L. W. Burger Jr., and D. P. Jones. 1998. "Breeding Ecology of Greater Prairie-Chickens (*Tympanuchus cupido*) in Relation to Prairie Landscape Configuration." *American Midland Naturalist* 140:111–21.

Samson, F., and F. Knopf. 1994. "Prairie Conservation in North America." *Bioscience* 44:418–21.

Sandercock, B. K., K. Martin, and G. Segelbacher, eds. 2011. *Ecology, Conservation, and Management of Grouse*. Berkeley: University of California Press.

Sands, L. 1939. *The Bird, the Gun, and the Dog*. New York: Carlyle House.

Sandys, E., and T. S. Van Dyke. 1924. *Upland Game Birds*. New York: Macmillan.

Sargeant, A. B., M. A. Sovada, and T. L. Shaffer. 1995. "Seasonal Predator Removal Relative to Hatch Rate of Duck Nests in Waterfowl Production Areas." *Wildlife Society Bulletin* 23(3): 507–13.

Schorger, A. W. 1944. "The Prairie-Chicken and Sharp-Tailed Grouse in Early Wisconsin." *Transactions of the Wisconsin Academy of Science, Arts and Letters* 35:1–59.

Schroeder, M. A. 1991. "Movement and Lek Visitation by Female Greater Prairie-Chickens in Relation to Predictions of Bradbury's Female Preference Hypothesis of Lek Evolution." *Auk* 108:896–903.

Schroeder, M. A., and R. K. Baydack. 2001. "Predation and the Management of Prairie Grouse." *Wildlife Society Bulletin* 29:24–32.

Schroeder, M. A., and L. A. Robb 1993. *Greater Prairie-Chicken*. The Birds of North America, No. 36.

Schwartz, C. W. 1945. *The Prairie Chicken in Missouri*. Columbia: University of Missouri Press and Missouri Conservation Commission.

Scott, W. E. 1947. "The Greater Prairie Chicken." *Wisconsin Conservation Bulletin* 12(1): 23–27.

Seton, E. T. 1891. *The Birds of Manitoba*. Washington, DC: Government Printing Office.

Shelford, V. E., and R. E. Yeatter. 1955. "Some Suggested Relations of Prairie Chicken Abundance to Physical Factors, Especially Rainfall and Solar Radiation." *Journal of Wildlife Management* 19(2): 233–42.

Silvy, N. J., M. J. Peterson, and R. R. Lopez. 2004. "The Cause of the Decline of Pinnated Grouse: The Texas Example." *Wildlife Society Bulletin* 32(1): 16–21.

Snyder, W. D. 1984. "Ring-Necked Pheasant Nesting Ecology and Wheat Farming on the High Plains." *Journal of Wildlife Management* 48(3): 878–88.

Snyder, J. W., E. C. Pelren, and J. A. Crawford. 1999. "Translocation Histories of Prairie Grouse in the United States." *Wildlife Society Bulletin* 27(2): 428–32.

Sovada, M., A. Sargeant, and J. Grier. 1995. "Differential Effects of Coyotes and Red Foxes on Duck Nest Success." *Journal of Wildlife Management* 59:1–9.

Sovada, M. A., M. C. Zicus, R. J. Greenwood, D. P. Rave, W. E. Newton, R. O. Woodward, and J. A. Beiser. 2000. "Relationship of Habitat Patch Size to Predator Community and Survival of Duck Nests." *Journal of Wildlife Management* 64(3): 820–31.

Stempel, M., and S. Rodgers. 1961. "History of Prairie Chickens in Iowa." *Proceedings of the Iowa Academy of Sciences* 68:314–22.

Stewart, O. C. 2002. *Forgotten Fires: Native Americans and the Transient Wilderness*. Norman: University of Oklahoma Press.

Stoddard, H. L. 1931. *The Bobwhite Quail: Its Habits, Preservation, and Increase*. New York: Charles Scribner's Sons.

Stohlgren, W. 2000. "Good Cow, Bad Cow: A Two-Headed Question over Cattle on the Range." *Nature Conservancy Magazine*, July–August, 12–19.

Svedarsky, W. D. 1988. "Reproductive Ecology of Female Greater Prairie-Chickens in Minnesota." In *Adaptive Strategies and Population Ecology of Northern Grouse*, vol. 1, edited by A. T. Bergerud and M. W. Gratson, 193–239. Minneapolis: University of Minnesota Press.

Svedarsky, W. D., R. L. Westemeier, R. J. Robel, S. Gough, and J. E. Toepfer. 2000. "Status and Management of the Greater Prairie-Chicken *Tympanuchus cupido pinnatus* in North America." *Wildlife Biology* 6(4): 277–84.

Svedarsky, W. D., T. J. Wolfe, and J. E. Toepfer. 1999. "Status and Management of the Greater Prairie Chicken in Minnesota." In *The Greater Prairie Chicken: A National Look*, edited by W. D. Svedarsky, R. H. Hier, and N. J. Silvy, 25–38. Minnesota Agricultural Experiment Station Miscellaneous Publication 99-1999. Saint Paul: University of Minnesota.

Swanson, E. B. 2007. *The Use and Conservation of Minnesota Wildlife*. Saint Paul: Minnesota Department of Natural Resources.

Symstad, A., E. Siemann, and J. Haarstad. 2000. "An Experimental Test of the Effect of Plant Functional Group on Arthropod Diversity." *Oikos* 89:243–53.

Syrowitz, J. 2013. "Brood Habitat and Invertebrate Biomass of the Greater Prairie Chicken (*Tympanuchus cupido pinnatus*) in Northwestern Minnesota." Master's thesis, University of Manitoba, Canada.

Toepfer, J. E. 2003. *Prairie Chickens and Grasslands: 2000 and Beyond*. Society of Tympanuchus cupido pinnatus.

———. 2006. "Status and Management of the Greater Prairie-Chicken in Wisconsin: 2006." *Passenger Pigeon* 69(3): 259–88.

Tokumoto, J., M. Danjo, Y. Kobayashi, K. Kinoshita, T. Omotehara, A. Tatsumi, M. Hashiguchi, et al. 2013. "Effects of Exposure to Chothianidin on the Reproductive System of Male Quails." *Journal of Veterinary Medical Science* 75(6): 755–60.

Towne, E., D. Hartnett, and R. Cochran. 2005. "Vegetation Trends in Tall-grass Prairie from Bison and Cattle Grazing." *Ecological Applications* 15(5): 1550–59.

Van den Bussche, R. A., S. R. Hoofer, D. A. Wiedenfeld, D. H. Wolfe, and S. K. Sherrod. 2003. "Genetic Variation within and among Fragmented Populations of Lesser Prairie-Chickens (*Tympanuchus pallidicinctus*)." *Molecular Ecology* 12:675–83.

Van Tramp, J. C. 1868. *Prairie and Rocky Mountain Adventures or Life in the West*. Columbus, OH: Segner and Condit.

Vinton, M., D. Hartnett, E. Finck, and J. Briggs. 1993. "Interactive Effects of Fire, Bison (*Bison bison*) Grazing, and Plant Community Composition in Tallgrass Prairie." *American Midland Naturalist* 129:10–18.

Walk, J. W., and R. E. Warner. 1999. "Effects of Habitat Area on the Occurrence of Grassland Birds in Illinois." *American Midland Naturalist* 141:339–44.

Walker, J., J. Rotella, J. Schmidt, C. Loesch, R. Reynolds, M. Lindberg, J. Ringelman, and S. Stephens. 2013. "Distribution of Duck Broods Relative to Habitat Characteristics in the Prairie Pothole Region. *Journal of Wildlife Management* 77(2): 392–404.

Westemeier, R. L. 1971. *The History and Ecology of Prairie Chickens in Central Wisconsin*. Research Bulletin No. 281. University of Wisconsin.

———. 1985. "The History of Prairie-Chickens and Their Management in Illinois." In *Selected Papers in Illinois History*, edited by R. W. McCluggage. Selected Papers in Illinois History 1983. Fourth Annual Illinois History Symposium of the Illinois State Historical Society.

———. 1997. "Grassland for Prairie Chickens: How Much Is Enough?" *Illinois Natural History Survey Reports* 343:1, 8.

Westemeier, R. L., J. D. Braun, S. A. Simpson, T. L. Esker, R. W. Jansen, J. W. Walk, E. L. Kerschner, et al. 1998. "Tracking the Long-Term Decline and Recovery of an Isolated Population." *Science* 282:1695–98.

Westemeier, R. L., J. E. Buhnerkempe, W. R. Edwards, J. D. Brawn, and S. A. Simpson. 1998. "Parasitism of Greater Prairie-Chicken Nests by Ring-Necked Pheasants." *Journal of Wildlife Management* 62:854–63.

Westemeier, R. L., and W. E. Edwards. 1987. "Prairie-Chickens: Survival in the Midwest." In *Restoring America's Wildlife*. US Department of the Interior, US Fish and Wildlife Service.

Westemeier, R. L., S. A. Simpson, and T. L. Esker. 1999. "Status and Management of 581 Greater Prairie Chickens in Illinois." In *The Greater Prairie Chicken: A National Look*, edited by W. D. Svedarsky, R. H. Hier, and N. J.

Silvy, 143–52. Minnesota Agricultural Experiment Station Miscellaneous
Publication 99-1999. Saint Paul: University of Minnesota.

Whitmore, R. W., K. P. Pruess, and R. E. Gold. 1986. "Insect Food Selection
by 2-Week-Old Ring-Necked Pheasant Chicks." *Journal of Wildlife Management* 50(2): 223–28.

Wilson, A. 1839. *American Ornithology*. New York: C. L. Cornish.

Winder, V. L., L. B. McNew, A. J. Gregory, L. M. Hunt, S. M. Wisely, and
B. K. Sandercock. 2013. "Effects of Wind Energy Development on Survival
of Female Greater Prairie-Chickens." *Journal of Applied Ecology* 51:395–405.

———. 2014. "Space Use by Female Greater Prairie-Chickens in Response to
Wind Energy Development." *Ecosphere* 5(1): 1–17.

Winter, M., and J. Faaborg. 1999. "Patterns of Area Sensitivity in Grassland-Nesting Birds." *Conservation Biology* 13(6): 1424–36.

Winter, M., D. H. Johnson, and J. A. Shaffer. 2006. "Does Body Size Affect
a Bird's Sensitivity to Patch Size and Landscape Structure?" *Condor*
108:808–16.

Winter, M., D. H. Johnson, J. A. Shaffer, T. M. Donovan, and W. D. Svedarsky. 2006. "Patch Size and Landscape Effects on Density and Nesting
Success of Grassland Birds." *Journal of Wildlife Management* 70(1): 158–72.

Wisdom, M. J., and L. S. Mills. 1997. "Sensitivity Analysis to Guide Population Recovery: Prairie-Chickens as an Example." *Journal of Wildlife Management* 61(2): 302–12.

Wisdom, M. J., L. S. Mills, and D. F. Doak. 2000. "Life Stage Simulation Analysis: Estimating Vital-Rate Effects on Population Growth for Conservation." *Ecology* 81(3): 628–41.

Wolfe, D. H. 2006. "Don't Fence Them In: For Prairie-Chickens, Airspace is
Habitat, Too." *Grouse Partnership News* 7:20–21, 29.

Wolfe, D. H., M. A. Patten, and S. K. Sherrod. 2009. "Reducing Grouse Collision Mortality by Marking Fences (Oklahoma)." *Ecological Restoration*
27:141–43.

Wolfe, W. M. 1890. "The Prairie Chicken of America." In *Upland Tales*, edited
by W. Mathewson, 8–15. Long Beach, CA: Safari Press.

Yeatter, R. E. 1943. "The Prairie Chicken in Illinois." *Natural History Survey
Bulletin* 22(4): 377–416.

———. 1963. "Population Responses of Prairie Chickens to Land-Use Change
in Illinois." *Journal of Wildlife Management* 27(4): 739–57.

Index

Hungarian partridge, 7
hunting, 51–55

insects, 35, 100

kin selection, 28

land use/cover, 68, 100
landscapes, 95
lek, 21–31; definition of, 25–26
lesser prairie-chicken, 5

mating display, 2; success, 28
metapopulation, 86, 88
Minnesota, 8, 44–45
Minnesota River, 6

natural selection, 27
nests: cover, 37; fire, 33–34; grass, 35;
    parasitism, 38–39, 92; survival, 57,
    62–64, 97
nicknames, 3

pampas, 11
parasites, 27, 60, 84
passenger pigeon, 9, 81
pesticides, 77–80; neonicotinoids,
    78–80
pheasant, 2, 7, 9, 10, 39, 59, 74, 92
pinnae, 2–3
plow, 43, 71
population, 58–70, 81–94; effective, 89
prairie: extinction, 18; fear of, 18;
    range/extent/boundaries, 16;
    restoration, 19–20
predation, 60–63, 76, 96–97

ptarmigan, 2

quail, 2, 10, 95

rainfall, 16
range, 41–50
reintroductions, 91–93
roots, 18

sage grouse, 5, 63
settlement, 2, 41
sexual selection, 26–27
sharp-tailed grouse, 5–7, 81
Smokey the Bear, 71
soils, 17
steppe, 11
survival, 57–59

towns, presence in, 8
Transeau, Edgar, 12
translocations. *See* reintroductions
trapping, 51–54, 63–65
trees. *See* forest
turbine, 76–77
turkey, 2

umbrella species, 105

veldt, 11

weather, 60, 65–66, 82–83
wilderness, 8
wind energy. *See* turbine
wires, telegraph and utility, 71, 74–75
working lands, 100

Other Bur Oak Books of Interest